The Supreme Self

Other books by S. Abhayananda

History Of Mysticism
The Wisdom Of Vedanta
Jnaneshvar: The Life And Works
Dattatreya: The Song Of The Avadhut
Thomas á Kempis: On The Love Of God

The Supreme Self

(2nd Revised Edition)

by S. Abhayananda

ATMA BOOKS
Olympia, Wash.

The Supreme Self (2nd Revised Edition)

Copyright © 1984, 1998 by Swami Abhayananda

Swami Abhayananda
ATMA BOOKS
3430 Pacific Ave. S.E.
Suite A-6144
Olympia, WA 98501

Library of Congress Cataloging -in -Publication Data

Abhayananda, Swami, 1938-
    The supreme self / by S. Abhayananda. -- 2nd rev. ed.
       p. cm.
    Includes bibliographical references (p. 182).
    ISBN 0-914557-10-6
    1. Spiritual life. 2. Self. 3. Abhayananda, Swami, 1938-
I. Title.
BL625.A3 1998
291.4'2--dc21
                          97-21590
                          CIP

In Thy Praise

And To Thy Glory

CONTENTS

CONTENTS
(Continued)

PART FOUR:
THE WORSHIP OF THE SELF

ACKNOWLEDGEMENTS

I wish to express my sincere gratitude to:
Rom Landau and George Allen & Unwin of London for permission to reprint extracts from *The Philosophy Of Ibn Arabi*; David Bohm, Basil Hiley and *Foundations Of Physics* magazine for permission to quote from the article, "*On The Intuitive Understanding Of Non-Locality As Implied By Quantum Theory*"; and William de Barry and Columbia University Press for permission to reprint the poem of Dara Shikoh from *Sources Of Indian Tradition*.

In addition, I would like to express a special thanks to Anne Hamilton-Byrne, without whose unselfish generosity and warm hospitality this book would not have been possible, and to Greg Bogart for his helpful suggestions and for his generous spirit.

JNTRODUCTJON

This book is intended to serve as an introduction to the knowledge of the supreme Self. The supreme Self of everyone is the universal Consciousness, or God. And it is the direct attainment of this knowledge which has revolutionized the lives of the great religious teachers throughout history, and which constitutes the one common thread which binds together all the great religious and philosophical traditions which have existed since time began. And yet today, though many thousands of extremely intelligent and devout men and women throughout history have experienced the direct knowledge of the supreme Self, the vast majority of human beings in the world are either unaware that such knowledge is possible, or are indifferent to it.

That the truth of all existence is experienceable, that the mystery of the Self and the universe is penetrable and subject to certainty, is not so well known as it should be, it seems to me. Nor is it so fully acknowledged as it ought to be that this universally experienced realization of the supreme Self is a reliable source of knowledge, applicable to a concise formulation of the nature of reality.

I have attempted, in this book, to explain the knowledge of the Self in a manner as thorough as possible from a number of different perspectives: firstly, from the perspective of my own direct experience, and then from the perspectives of various branches of knowledge. I have examined the mystical theologies of several major religious traditions and have attempted to show that, aside from the difference in languages and terminologies, they are identical.

I have also carefully examined the views of contemporary scientists, whose discoveries during the past century have had so profound a bearing on our understanding of the nature of reality, and I have tried to show that the great gap that once existed between the world-view of science and that of mysticism is gone; that, in fact, the time is not far distant when it must be universally acknowledged that these two disciplines, though utilizing different methodologies, are in complete agreement.

In order to provide a broad comprehensive look at the ancient yet ever new knowledge of the Self, I have drawn from a wide variety of sources: mystics, philosophers, scientists, astrologers, and saints. And while I have presented the knowledge of the supreme Self from many different viewpoints, it is my own subjective experience of the Self which is the core and foundation of my certainty, and the impetus for my effort to communicate it. It is my greatest hope that, for some few at least, this book will open a door of understanding through which a ray of light may shine upon the eternal verities.

S. Abhayananda

PART ONE:

The Experience Of The Self

"The knower of Brahman becomes Brahman."

-- *Mundaka Upanishad*

the universe. I could not help feeling that there had been a tacit conspiracy in the Western world by the church, the state, and academia to conceal from me the fact that God could be "seen" and known. But, of course, the truth of the matter is that the knowledge was always there; only I was simply not ready to grasp these ideas until this moment, and it was only now that I was able to comprehend what the *Upanishads* had to tell:

> He is beyond time and space, and yet He is the God of infinite forms who dwells in our inmost thoughts, and who is seen by those who love Him.[1]

> He cannot be seen by the eye, and words cannot reveal Him. He cannot be reached by the senses, or by austerity or sacred actions. By the grace of wisdom and purity of mind, He can be seen indivisible in the silence of contemplation.[2]

> He is the Eternal among things that pass away, pure Consciousness of conscious beings, the One who fulfills the prayers of many. Only the wise who see Him in their souls attain the peace eternal.[3]

Reading through the collection of writings known as the *Upanishads*, I had a sense of recognition, a recollection of truths I had known before. "Of course, of course," I kept repeating as I devoured the words of the sages. Nothing in the Western cultural tradition came close to the penetrating subtlety and clarity of the writings of these ancient Indian seers who had penned these immortal scriptures.

But the West *did* have its seers -- though they do not appear as early or as abundantly as their Eastern counterparts. In the West, the experience of Unity, "the vision of God," is only vaguely implied by the early Greek philosophers such as Heraclitus, Pythagorus, and Socrates (by way of Plato). The later Stoics and Philo of Alexandria in the 1st century C.E. also refer only vaguely to such an experience, without any real attempt to offer a convincing account. In fact, it is not until Plotinus (204-270 C.E.) that an explicit and unequivocal account of "the vision of God" is offered in the West. Here is Plotinus' description of his own experience in an extensive passage from his *Enneads*:

> The soul naturally loves God and yearns to be one with Him, just as a noble daughter naturally loves her noble father. ... And suddenly, [she] is uplifted and sees, without ever knowing how; ... the Supreme has come to her, or rather has revealed Its presence. She has turned away from everything around her and has readied herself, having made herself as beautiful as possible and fashioned herself in likeness with the Divine by those preparations and adornments which come unsought to those who grow ready for the vision. And she has seen that Divine presence suddenly manifesting within herself, for now there is nothing between herself and the Divine. There is now no longer a duality, but a two-in-one; for, so long as that presence continues, all distinction between them is dissolved. The longing of a lover to unite with his [human] beloved is a longing for a mere imitation of that Divine and perfect union.
>
> ... In this state of absorbed contemplation, there is no longer a relationship between a subject and an object; the vision itself is the one continuous Being, so that seeing and seen are one thing; the object and the act of vision have become identical ...
>
> ... It is a knowing of the Self restored to its original purity. No doubt we should not speak of *seeing*; but we cannot help speaking in terms of duality, such as "the seer"

and "the seen," instead of asserting boldly that it is the attainment of absolute Unity. In this *seeing*, we neither regard an object nor perceive distinctions; for there are not two. The man is altered, no longer himself nor belonging to himself; he is merged with the Supreme, sunken into It, one with It. ... Duality exists only in separation; by our holding ourselves apart from It, the Supreme is set outside of us. This is why the vision cannot be described; we cannot separate the Supreme from ourselves to speak of It, for if we have seen something separate and distinct, we have fallen short of the Supreme which can be known only as one with oneself.

... [In this vision] there are not two; beholder is one with the beheld ... The man who has experienced this mingling with the Supreme must -- if he but recalls It -- carry the memory of Divinity impressed upon his soul. He is become the Unity, and nothing within him or without can create any diversity. Nor is there any movement now, or passion, or outreaching desire, once this ascent is attained. Reasoning is suspended and all intellection as well, and even -- to dare the word -- the very *self* is gone. Filled with God, he has in perfect stillness attained isolation, aloneness.

... This is the life of the gods and of the godlike and blessed among men, ...the passing of the alone to the Alone.[4]

After Plotinus, perhaps the most lucid and explicit description of the experience of Unity comes from the 13th century German mystic, the Dominican Prior of Erfurt, Meister Eckhart (1260-1327). Eckhart's Sermons and other writings were "condemned" by the Catholic Church in 1329; nonetheless, his writings have carried the torch of mystical experience over the centuries by which the way of many later mystics has been lighted. Speaking of his own experience of Unity, Meister Eckhart declares:

In this breaking through [of consciousness], I find that
God and I are both the same. Then I am what I [always]
was; I neither wax nor wane, for I am the motionless
Cause that is moving all things. [5]

I am converted into Him in such a way that He makes
me one being with Himself -- not a *similar* being. By the
living God, it is true that there is no distinction. [6]

The eye by which I see God is the same as the eye by
which God sees me. My eye and God's eye are one and
the same--one in seeing, one in knowing, and one in loving. [7]

Here, one cannot speak of the soul anymore, for she
has lost her nature yonder in the oneness of divine essence.
There, she is no longer called soul, but is called
immeasurable Being. [8]

I found in me all things forgotten, my own self
forgotten and awareness of Thee, alone, O God. ... I found
myself with Thee, being Thy being and speaking the Word
and breathing the spirit. [9]

Here and there, I found other seers scattered along the
shores of time, from legendary eras to the present: early
Greek philosophers, sages from the Vedic period of India,
Moslem Sufis, Christians, Chinese Taoists and Buddhists;
each telling the experience of Unity in terms that reflect
the time and tradition in which he or she wrote. The
women, in most cases, tended to color their accounts with
emotion and allegory, but it was clear that the experience
had occurred in them, and obviously showed no sexual bias.
In fact, it appeared that all sorts of people had experienced
the vision of Unity; not only those who could express it in
philosophical or poetical terms, but also simple good-
hearted people who have left us no record of their
experience.

Of those who wrote, who recorded for posterity some of the insights gained in that vision of truth, were many who said little or nothing of the experience itself, but confined themselves to presenting a systematic philosophy based on that experience; others, like the prophets of early Judaism, wrote or spoke as "holy" men, feeling that they were chosen to be spokesmen for God. And some, like the Buddha and the yogis, in an effort to stem a tide of futile intellectual speculation, declined to speak at all of the traditional notions of God, soul, and the nature of reality, but stressed instead the need to practice those disciplines which would lead to the direct experience of Truth, wherein all doubts and speculations would be resolved.

Naturally, each of these great beings spoke in his own language, his own restricted terminology, and the consequence is that today we regard each of these efforts to reveal the nature of reality as disparate and unrelated "philosophies" or "religions." But the experience of Reality is the same for all, of course; and in all the declarations of the many prophets and Messiahs one can hear the attempt to convey a common knowledge based on that common vision.

It was thus I passed my days in the forest, devouring the writings of the sages and saints of the world in whose company I found great comfort and happiness. During the day I read, and in the evenings I sat quietly, happily, in the presence of God. The growing clarity of my understanding seemed to open my heart to His ever-present reality, and little by little, I grew more aware of and filled by His Love. My intellectual curiosity had been satisfied; and now there remained only the simple directing of all my attention, all my thought, to the God whom I desired with all my heart.

The author, Spring, 1966

My cabin in the woods

3. ENLIGHTENMENT

But it was not all sunshine and light. My little cabin in the redwoods was cool in the summer, but damp in the winter, as I discovered that first winter in '66. The little babbling brook swelled to a cascading Colorado river in my backyard, and I had to catch water coming down the slope from the road in little waterfalls to get clear water for drinking or cooking. I sat close to the cast-iron cooking stove, with the little side door open so I could watch the dancing blue and gold flames sizzle the oak logs and turn them to glowing ash.

Day and night, during the California winter, the rain drizzled outside the window in a steady, grey, time-dissolving continuum. I sat dully in the canvas chair by the stove, calling inwardly, "Hari! Hari!" In the mornings, I'd prepare oatmeal and a bath by the stove; I'd pour hot water from a pitcher over my body onto the concrete floor, and then sweep it outside. The rain would stop sometimes during the day, and then I would go out and walk the once dusty logging roads through the woods and up through the meadows in the high ground. "Hari! Hari! Hari!" was my continual call.

The dark skies kept my energies subdued, and my mind indrawn. My days passed uneventfully. It was in the night that the embers of my heart began to glow keenly as I sat in the dark, watching the fire contained in the stove. A stillness -- sharp-edged and intense -- filled my cabin and I spoke very closely, very intimately, with the God who had drawn me there. And He would sometimes speak to me in the stillness of the night, while I wrote down His words.

Hari became my only thought, my only love. And while the days and nights became endless stretches of greyness, wetness, my mind became brighter and brighter with an intense light that displayed every wandering thought that arose as a compelling drama in bold technicolor and panavision; and then I would pull my mind back with "Hari!" I had realized that I could have or become whatever I settled for in my mind; and I was determined to refuse every inspiration that was not God Himself. I was steadfastly resolved to refuse all envisualizations, all mental wanderings, holding my mind in continual remembrance and longing for Hari alone.

In the nights, my wakefulness burned like a laser of intensely focused yearning, a penetrating, searching lighthouse of hope in the black interior of the cabin, as I witnessed the play of the flickering flames dying out in the stove's interior. On one such night, I lit a candle; a song was being written in my notebook, and I was understanding very clearly, very vividly, just what it was that I loved, what it was that I was pledging my life to:

> Thou art Love, and I shall follow all Thy ways.
> I shall have no care, for Love cares only to love.
> I shall have no fear, for Love is fearless;
> Nor shall I frighten any, for Love comes sweetly
>   and meek.
> I shall keep no violence within me,
> Neither in thought nor in deed, for Love comes
>   peacefully.
> I shall bear no shield or sword,
> For the defense of Love is love.
> I shall seek Thee in the eyes of men,
> For love seeks Thee always.
> I shall keep silence before Thine enemies,

And lift to them Thy countenance,
For all are powerless before Thee.
I shall keep Thee in my heart with precious care,
Lest Thy light be extinguished by the winds;
For without Thy light, I am in darkness.
I shall go free in the world with Thee --
Free of all bondage to anything but Thee --
For Thou art my God, the sole Father of my being,
The sweet breath of Love that lives in my heart;
And I shall follow Thee, and live with Thee,
And lean on Thee till the end of my days.

November 18, 1966:

This was the night I was to experience God. This was the night I learned who I am. All day long the rain had been dripping outside my cabin window. And now the silent night hovered around me. I sat motionless, watching the dying coals in the stove. "Hari!" my mind called in the wakeful silence of my interior. During the whole day, I had felt my piteous plight so sorrowfully, so maddeningly; "Dear Lord, all I want is to die in Thee," I cried within myself. "I have nothing, no desire, no pleasure in this life -- but in Thee. Won't you come and take this worthless scrap, this feeble worm of a soul, back into Thyself!"

"O Father," I cried, "listen to my prayer! I am Thine alone. Do come and take me into Thy heart. I have no other goal, but Thee and Thee alone."

Then I became very quiet. I sat emptied, but very awake, listening to God's silence. I balanced gingerly, quakingly, on the still clarity of nothingness. I became aware that I was scarcely breathing. My breath was very shallow, nearly imperceptible -- close to the balance point, where it would become non-existent. And my eyes peered into the darkness with a wide-eyed intensity that amazed me. I knew my pupils must be very large. I felt on the brink of a meeting with absolute clearness of mind. I hovered there, waiting. And then, from somewhere in me, deeper that I knew even existed, a prayer came forth that, I sensed, must have been installed in my heart at the moment of my soul-birth in the mind of God: "Dear God, let me be one with Thee, not that I might glory in Thy love, but that I might speak out in Thy praise and to Thy glory for the benefit of all Thy children."

It was then, in that very moment, that the veil fell away. Something in me changed. Suddenly I *knew*; I experienced infinite Unity. And I thought, "Of course; it's been me all the time! Who else could I possibly be!" I lit a candle, and by the light of the flickering flame, while seated at the card table in my little cabin, I transmitted to paper what I was experiencing in eternity. Here is the "Song" that was written during that experience (the commentaries in parentheses which follow each verse were added much later):

O my God, even this body is Thine own!

> (*Suddenly I knew that this entity which I call my body was God's own, was not separate from God, but was part of the continuous ocean of Consciousness; and I exclaimed in my heart, "O my God, even this body is Thine own!" There was no longer any me distinct from that one Consciousness; for that illusion was now dispelled.*)

Though I call to Thee and seek Thee amidst
    chaos,
Even I who seemed an unclean pitcher
    amidst Thy waters --
Even I am Thine own.

*(Heretofore, I had called to God in the chaos of a
multitude of thoughts, a multitude of voices and motions
of mind -- the very chaos of hell. And in my calling, I
was as though standing apart from God; I felt myself to
be an unclean pitcher immersed in the ocean of God,
dividing the waters within from the water without.
Though God was in me and God was without, there
had still remained this illusion of 'me'. But now the
idea of a separating 'ego' was gone. And I was aware
that I -- this whole conglomerate of body, mind,
consciousness, which I call "I" -- am none else but that
One, and belong to that One, besides whom there is
nothing.)*

Does a wave cease to be of the ocean?

*(A wave is only a form that arises out of the ocean
and is nothing but ocean. In the same way, my form was
as a wave of pure Consciousness, of pure God. How had
I imagined it to be something else? And yet it was that
very ignorance that had previously prevented me from
seeing the truth.)*

Do the mountains and the gulfs cease to be of the
    earth?

*(Mountains and valleys in relation to the earth,
like waves in relation to the ocean, seem to have an
independent existence, an independent identity; yet*

they are only irregularities, diverse forms, of the earth itself.)

Or does a pebble cease to be stone?

(A pebble is, of course, nothing but stone -- just as I now realized in growing clarity that I was none else but the one 'stuff' of Existence. Even though I seemed to be a unique entity separate from the rest of the universe, I was really a piece of the universal Reality, as a pebble is really a piece of stone.)

How can I escape Thee?
Thou art even That which thinks of
    escape!

(Thought too is a wave on the ocean of God. The thought of separation -- can that be anything but God? The very tiniest motion of the mind is like the leaping of the waves on the ocean of Consciousness, and the fear of leaping clear of the ocean is a vain one for the wave. That which thinks of separation is that very Consciousness from which there can never ever be any separation. That One contains every- thing within It. So, what else could I, the thinker, be?)

Even now, I speak the word, "Thou," and
    create duality.

(Here, now, as I write, as I think of God and speak to Him as "Thou," I am creating a duality between myself and God where no duality exists in truth. It is the creation of the mind. Having habituated itself to separation, the mind creates an "I" and a "Thou," and thus experiences duality.)

I love, and create hatred.

(Just as for every peak there's a valley, so the thought of love that arises in the mind has, as its valley, as its opposite, hatred. The impulse of the one creates the other, as the creation of a north pole automatically creates a south pole, or as "beauty" necessitates "ugliness," or as "up" brings along with it "down," or as "ahead" gives birth to "behind." The nature of the mind is such that it creates a world of duality where only the One actually is.)

I am in peace, and am fashioning chaos.

(The very nature of God's phenomenal creation is also dual; His cosmic creation alternates from dormant to dynamic, while He, Himself, remains forever unchanging. In the same way, while our consciousness remains unmoved, the mind is in constant alternation. For example, when it is stilled, it is like a spring compressed, representing potential dynamic release. The mind's peace, therefore, is itself the very mother of its activity.)

Standing on the peak, I necessitate the depths.

(Just as the peak of the wave necessitates the trough of the wave [since you can't have one without the other], wakefulness necessitates sleep, good necessitates its opposite. Exultation in joy is paid for with despair; they are an inseparable pair.)

But now, weeping and laughing are gone;
Night is become day.

(Now I am experiencing the transcendent "stillness" of the One, where this alternation, this duality, of which creation is made, is no more. It is a clear awareness that all opposites are derived from the same ONE, and are therefore dissolved. Laughing and its opposite, weeping, are the peak and the trough which have become levelled in the stillness of the calmed ocean, the rippleless surface of the waters of Consciousness. Night and day have no meaning here: All is eternity.)

Music and silence are heard as one.

(Sound, silence -- both are contained in the eternal Consciousness which cannot be called silent, which cannot be called sound; It produces all sounds, yet, as their source, It is silence. Both are united in the One of which they consist.)

My ears are all the universe.

(There is only Me. Even the listening is Me.)

All motion has ceased;
Everything continues.

(The activity of the universe does not exist for Me, yet everything is still in motion as before. It is only that I am beyond both motion and non-motion. For I am the Whole; all motion is contained in Me, yet I Myself am unmoving.)

Life and death no longer stand apart.

(From where I am, the life and death of individual beings is less than a dream -- so swiftly generations rise and fall, rise and fall! Whole eons of creation pass like a dream in an instant; where then are life and death? How do they differ? They too are but an artificial duality that is resolved in the One timeless Self.)

No I, no Thou;
No now, or then.

(There is no longer a reference "I" that refers to a separate individual entity; there is no longer anything separate to refer to as "Thou." This one knowing Consciousness which is I is all that exists or ever existed. Likewise, there is no 'now' or 'then', for time pertains only to the dream and has no meaning here beyond all manifestation.)

Unless I move, there is no stillness.

(Stillness, too, is but a part of duality, bringing into existence motion. Motion and stillness, the ever-recurring change, are the dream constituents in the dream of duality! Stillness without motion cannot be. Where I am, neither of these exists.)

Nothing to lament, nothing to vanquish;

(Lament? In the pure sky of infinity, who is there to lament? What is there to doubt? Where there is no other, but only this One, what error or obstacle could there be? What is there to stand in the way of infinity? What is there other than Me?)

Nothing to pride oneself on --

All is accomplished in an instant.

(Pride belongs only to man, that tiny doll, that figment of imagination who, engrossed in the challenge of conflict with other men, prides himself on his petty accomplishments. Here, whole universes are created in an instant and destroyed, and everything that is accomplished is accomplished by the One. Where, then, is pride?)

All may now be told without effort.

(Here am I, with a view to the Eternal, and my hand writing in the world of creation, in the world of men. What a wonderful opportunity to tell all to eager humanity! Everything is known without the least effort. Let me tell it, let me share it, let me reveal it!)

Where is there a question?

(But see! Where everything is very simply and obviously Myself, what question could there be? Here, the possibility of a question cannot arise. Who could imagine a more humorous situation?)

Where is the temple?

(What about explaining the secrets of the soul, and how it is encased in that temple of God called 'the body?' That secret does not exist; for, when all is seen and experienced as one Being, where is that which may be regarded as the receptacle, the temple?)

Which the Imperishable?

Which the abode?

*(Which may I call the imperishable God, the
Eternal? And which may I call the vessel in which
God exists and lives? Consciousness does not perish.
The Energy of which this body consists does not
perish. All is eternal; there is no differentiation
here.)*

I am the pulse of the turtle;
I am the clanging bells of joy.

*(I am everywhere; I am life! I am the very
heart-beat of even the lowliest of creatures. It is I
who surge in the heart as joy, as surging joy like the
ecstatic abandonment of clanging bells.)*

I bring the dust of blindness;
I am the fire of song.

*(I am the cause of man's ignorance of Me, yet it
is I who leap in his breast as the exultation of song.)*

I am in the clouds and I am in the gritty soil;
In pools of clear water my image is found.

*(I am that billowing beauty in the sky; I play in
all these forms! And the gritty soil which produces
the verdure of the earth -- I am that soil, that black
dirt. I am every tiny pebble of grit, cool and moist.
And when, as man, I lean over the water, I discover
My image, and see Myself shining in My own eyes.)*

I am the dust on the feet of the wretched,
The toothless beggars of every land.

*(I live in the dust that covers the calloused feet
of those thin, ragged holy men who grin happily at
you as you pass them by.)*

I have given sweets that decay to those who
    crave them;
I have given my wealth unto the poor and
    lonely.

*(Each of my manifestations, according to their
understanding, receives whatever they wish of the
transitory pleasures of the world; but the wealth of
My peace, My freedom, My joy, I give to those who
seek no other wealth, who seek no other joy, but Me.)*

My hands are open -- nothing is
    concealed.

*(I have displayed all My wealth; according to
his evolution, his wisdom, each chooses what he will
have in this life.)*

All things move together of one accord;
Assent is given throughout the universe to
    every falling grain.

*(All is one concerted whole; everything works
together, down to the tiniest detail, in the flower-like
unfoldment of this world. All is the doing of the
One.)*

The Sun stirs the waters of My heart,
And the vapor of My love flies to the four
    corners of the world.

*(Like a thousand-rayed sunburst of joy, My love
showers forth as the universe of stars and planets
and men. And then, this day of manifestation gives
way to the night of dissolution ...)*

The Moon stills Me, and the cold darkness is My
    bed.

*(And the universe withdraws into My utter
darkness of stillness and rest.)*

I have but breathed, and everything is
    rearranged
And set in order once again.

*(The expansion and contraction of this entire
universe is merely an out-breath and an in-breath;
a mere sigh.)*

A million worlds begin and end in every
    breath,

*(And, flung out into the endless reaches of
infinity, worlds upon worlds evolve, enact their
tumultous dramas, and then withdraw from the
stage once more. This cycle repeats itself again and
again; the universe explodes from a single mass,
expands as gas, and elements form. Eventually they
become living organisms, which evolve into intelligent
creatures, culminating in man. And one by one
each learns the secret that puts an end to their*

game. And again, the stars reach the fullness of their course; again everything is drawn back to its source, ...

And, in this breathing, all things are sustained.

After this, I collapsed in bed, exhausted by the sheer strain of holding my mind on so keen an edge. When I awoke, it was morning. Immediately, I recalled the experience of the night before, and arose. I went outside to the sunlight, dazed and disoriented. I bent, and took up a handful of gravel, letting it slip slowly through my fingers. "I am in this?" I asked dumbfoundedly.

I felt as though I had been thrust back into a dream from which I had no power to awaken. My only thought was to return to that state I had known the night before. I rushed up the twisted road and scrambled up the hill to the cliff on top of the world, above the forest and ocean, where I had often conversed with God; and I sat there, out of breath, praying, with tears running down my cheeks, for Him to take me back into Himself. Before long, a chill blanket of grey fog, which had risen up from the ocean below, swept over me, engulfing me in a misty cloud. And after a few moments, I reluctantly went back, down the mountain.

4. THE WAVE
AND THE OCEAN

That magical night, while sitting there before the fire in my dark cabin, I had entered into 'the kingdom of God.' I had been privileged to 'see' into the real nature of myself and all existence. And I had seen clearly that my greater Self was the sole Source of everything. That *I* was the Life in all life, the one Existence manifest in all forms; and yet, that clarity had been all too brief, and I was once again separate and isolated, no longer aware of my greater Self, but projected back into a world of time and space, a world of separable forms.

After some time, I adjusted to the fact that I would have to live out my life in this dream-like world, and would need to learn to hold to the awareness of my eternal identity, my real Self, while living in this figmentary body. I was as though born anew; I was free to live as I chose, without fear, without concern. There were times when I ran naked with the deer on top of the mountain, and times when I sat in the hollow of a burned out redwood tree, listening to the rain, and wondering if I would die in such a lonely place without anyone ever knowing what I had known.

I foraged for dandelion greens along the roadsides, I gathered fallen lemons from beneath untended trees, I made soda bread in my skillet on the iron stove, and I carried sacks of perfect golden delicious apples from the orchard of one of my neighbor friends to lay on the windowsill of my back porch to store for the Spring. And there were cold clear Winter mornings when I'd stand in that picturesque orchard and make my joyful breakfast on ripe red figs that looked like strawberry jam when you broke them open.

For that first year, I had refused to touch money. Trusting entirely in God's mercy, I'd walk into town, pick a street, and knock on doors, offering to do whatever work I could do for a meal. This resulted in some unsavory and inadequate meals and led to my appreciation for the societal evolution from bartered trade to the monetary system. Thereafter, I accepted money for my services, and purchased my own preferred foodstuffs. But this too proved inadequate, as I needed more than sustenance; I needed to share my love and my gift of knowledge.

With that realization my life took on a new purpose. Several times a week I'd walk the ten miles to town and take my place for a couple of hours on the corner in front of the bookstore to hand out to passersby a small printed version of my 'Two Psalms.' I'd enter into a state of prayerful contemplation while standing there as a fool before everyone, and the sweetness that I felt for the universal Mother in evidence all about me shone on my face and drew people to approach, wondering what on earth this fool was passing out.

I felt that in these two songs -- one of love, one of union -- was the whole of the treasure I had been given, that they contained God's twofold message that I was born to deliver; and in those few years I handed out over two thousand of these little booklets to the pedestrians of Santa Cruz. I wore a slitted shoebox hung 'round my neck for donations, and with the nickels and dimes given to me I'd later purchase a bag of flour and perhaps a box of raisins, and then climb the long road back to my solitary cabin.

Other days, when I didn't go into town, there was always the need for wood; so, frequently, I'd spend the mornings dragging dry fir branches down from the hilltops to chop into kindling, or split oak rounds with my axe into stove-sized lengths of fuel. And in the hot afternoons, tired from my wood-gathering, I'd set up my card table outdoors and exult in the praise of God, marvelling at His Goodness and Beauty, as I ate my soda bread and sliced apple and lemonade in the shade of my peaceful forest home.

Life was good; I had the peace of my forest, the coolness of my cabin, and the satisfaction of delivering my gifts to others. Reflecting on my situation, I was very happy that I had attained what I had come to the forest to attain, and very grateful to God for His immense blessings. Each morning I awoke with His name on my lips, and His name filled my heart at night as I drifted off to sleep.

For four more winters I stayed, happy in my little cabin, but never again finding my way to that place of stillness where my greater Self lives. It seemed that my time of meeting with the Eternal had passed, and a time of preparation for the sharing of my knowledge was now pressing me forward, for it was to that I now felt my heart urging me. Life is never static, and the inevitable pull of destiny would eventually draw me out of my woods after nearly five years, and on to other lands, other adventures.

At some point it dawned on me that the fact that I had 'seen', had clearly *realized*, the absolute Truth of the universe was, and would always remain, of very little relevance to the rest of the world. Scientists would go on searching for clues to the nature of the universe, religious proponents would go on believing in their religious doctrines, atheists and agnostics would go on as unknowing as before.   Enlightenment, like all other experience, is individual and non-transferrable. Whatever I might say or do to pass this knowledge on to others, the *knowledge* was mine alone.   A concept, an understanding, could be transmitted perhaps, but *knowledge* could not; that required the same direct "seeing" which came to me.

How many others had sought to give the benefit of that liberating knowledge to the world, and to what avail? See what terrible misconceptions and misdirections have resulted from the attempt on the part of Moses, Jesus, the Buddha, al-Hallaj, Eckhart, and all those others to give expression to the knowledge of the one universal Self! Each of us may presumably benefit from the verbalized expression of the knowledge possessed by another, and may derive clarity and understanding of our own from those shared descriptions, but we cannot *know* the bliss of revelation, we cannot *experience* the inner perception of our eternal Identity unless It makes Itself known *to us.*

And so, I would tell of it; I would, as all those many others had done, tell everything I possibly could about It, but I knew that others could only believe or not believe, understand or remain incomprehending; that would be the most anyone could gain by my telling, for no one could really *know* until that inner experience made them to know.

I would tell of it because there was something in me which *had* to tell of it. From the moment I had been given that revelation, my life had no other meaning or purpose but to fulfill that longing in my soul that had expressed itself in my prayer: "Make me one with Thee, not that I might glory in Thy love, but that I might speak out in Thy praise and to Thy glory for the benefit of all Thy children."

Whether anyone would truly be benefitted or not, I had been shown the Truth, and I meant to speak of It.

But I would come to realize that the experience of Unity, shared by Jesus, the Buddha, Shankara, Plotinus, Eckhart, and many others, is impossible to describe; for to speak of It is to assert the paradox that the One is both an absolutely unchanging constant *and* the very substance of all phenomenal forms that we perceive as inconstant and changing. That the transcendent God and the temporal world are complementary aspects of one and the same Reality is not at all evident, and goes against the accepted Judeo-Christian mythology. To those who have never experienced that Unity, such declarations about It must appear illogical and self-contradictory. This apparent contradiction can be resolved and understood, however, if we recall the analogy of the wave and the ocean:

Imagine, for a moment, that there exists a wave who one day hears another wave speaking of "The Ocean, Lord of all the waves." And so, being intrigued, our wave sets out in search of this "Ocean." His search leads him to a wise old wave who advises him, "Look within, for the Ocean is within you." Then, one day, while concentrating within himself, and asking the Lord Ocean to reveal Himself, the wave suddenly awakens to the clear awareness that *he* is the Ocean. The Ocean, he realizes, is who he has always been, though he had identified with the limited wave-form. He realizes that he is the one reality that is manifesting as all the waves -- and yet, though the waves form and dissolve, and again form and dissolve, he, the Ocean-as-a-whole, remains the same, continually unchanged and unaffected. This is exactly what the mystic experiences in his awakening to the universal Self: he is one of the many

manifestations, but he is also the one Reality --
unchanging, eternal.

Shankaracharya, the great 8th century expounder of the
non-dualistic philosophy of Vedanta, called this apparent
duality between the many and the One, a "superimposition":

> Like ripples on the water, the worlds arise from,
> exist in and dissolve into the supreme Lord, who is the
> material cause and support of everything.
>
> The manifested world of plurality is superimposed
> upon the eternal, all-pervading Lord whose nature is
> Existence-Consciousness, just as bangles and bracelets
> are superimposed on gold. [1]

Various golden ornaments have their separate forms and
qualities, and yet, in the end, they are all only gold.

Another way of explaining the "superimposition" of the
phenomenal world on God is by analogy with the ordinary
experience of the superimposition of a thought or image
upon one's own consciousness. Notice, for a moment, how
a thought is superimposed upon the background of pure
mental awareness: it has a definite reality, albeit a
temporary one, and yet it does not mar or alter in any way
that background consciousness. The thought-form or
image and the background consciousness exist simultaneously, with a definite distinction between them; however,
the thought is formed not only *on* consciousness, but *of*
consciousness -- just as a wave is not only on, but of, the
ocean.

In a way identical to this, the phenomenal world of
forms is projected in and upon the supreme Consciousness:
the world and God are separate and distinct -- but the world

has no *independent* existence; it is formed not only on, but of, God. In the mystic's vision, one's body is recognized as a form whose substance is the universal substance, and one's consciousness is recognized as the only consciousness there is. And then one knows that he has no other identity, nor ever had any other, but the One, who alone is.

Though this realization was conceptualized in a rational form in the *Upanishads* of India long before such concepts were formulated anywhere else, there were undoubtedly some few in the Near East and West, even in ancient times, who had experienced this astounding revelation. However, there was as yet no language for speaking of it -- save the language of myth. For how was one to convey such knowledge? How was one to speak of a unitive Reality which is both One and many, both God and the universe? How could such a paradox be made acceptable to the philosophers, the scholars with their clever logic? How could it be possible to explain a God who creates without creating, who sets a universe within Himself in motion without ever moving or changing, who appears to be two -- God and universe -- and yet remains One?

It became apparent early on that what was needed was the introduction of two terms, each to designate one aspect of this dual-faceted Being, yet which would in no way represent two separate and distinct entities, but One -- a One with two facets. There was a need for one term to represent the absolute, unchanging Godhead, and another term to signify the creative aspect which manifests as the universe. Here's how each of the various religious traditions gave expression to this concept:

∞   ∞   ∞

PART TWO:

The Philosophy Of The Self

"The mystics' words appear in a hundred different forms, but if God is one and the Way is one, how can their words be other than one? They do appear in different guises, but in substance they are one."

-- Jalaluddin Rumi,
Discourses

1. VEDANTA

Let us first turn to India, and trace the beginnings of the duality-in-unity idea from one of the earliest scriptures of which we know: the time-worn *Vedas*. No one knows just when they were written, but scholars place this collection of poetic hymns and mystic lore in the second millennia B.C.E. The earliest of the *Vedas* (meaning "Wisdom") are from a time of the most primitive agrarian society, and reveal a simple tribal mentality which regards the awesome mysterious forces of the universe as temperamental gods. Later additions to the collection, however, reveal a developing sophistication, presaging the later development of the monistic philosophy of the *Upanishads*. It is in such later Vedic hymns that we find the seed of the Hindu version of duality-in-unity. Here in the *Creation Hymn* from the Rig Veda, an unknown sage describes the knowledge unveiled in mystical experience of the eternal Unity existing prior to manifestation:

1. Then, neither the non-Real (*asat*) nor the
        Real (*sat*) existed.
    There was no sky then, nor the heavens
        beyond it.
    What was contained by what, and where, and who
        sheltered it?
    What unfathomed depths, what cosmic
        ocean, existed then?

2. Then, neither death nor deathlessness
        existed;
    Between day and night there was as yet no
        distinction.

That ONE (*tad ekam*), by Its own power
(*svadha*) breathlessly breathed.

The author speaks of that unitive state wherein the
(apparent) duality of the subjective reality (*sat*) and the
transient objective universe (*asat*) does not exist; there is
only the undivided ONE. Then, he goes on to describe how
this initial division took place:

3. In the beginning, darkness lay wrapped in
    darkness;
    All was one undifferentiated (*apraketa*)
    sea (*salila*).
    Then, within that one undifferentiated
    Existence,
    [Something] arose by the heat of
    concentrated energy (*tapas*).

4. What arose in That in the beginning was
    Desire (*kama*),
    [Which is] the primal seed of mind
    (*manas*).
    The wise, having searched deep within
    their own being,
    Have perceived the (unitive) bond
    (*bandha*) between the Real (*sat*) and the
    unreal (*asat*). [1]

Desire, springing up within the One undifferentiated
Being, gave rise to mind; i.e., the production of thought, and
that thought, made manifest as the universe, brings about
the duality of the subject (the eternally witnessing
consciousness) and the object (the world of form). Both
exist at once: the pure unmoving Consciousness and the
incessantly evolving universe. And yet, though there is an

apparent duality, it is an illusory duality; and therefore, the Unity remains undisturbed.

Though they are not two, the transcendent Reality is the Source and essence of the projected universe. This is the bond between the Real (the Eternal) and the unreal (the temporal) which is seen by those seers who search deep within themselves. If you wish to understand it, take note of your own consciousness and its projection of thought upon itself. It is both the unmoving witness and the active parade of images. This play of duality goes on within you, and yet you remain always one, undivided.

Those who have experienced this Unity say that during that experience it is realized that "all motion has ceased"; and yet at the same time, "everything continues." In other words, while all this thought-produced universe remains in motion, at its Source there is nothing but infinite peace. This paradox was also expressed by the author of the *Isha Upanishad*:

> It moves; It moves not.
> It is far, and It is near.
> It is within all this,
> And It is outside of all this. [2]

But how is such a paradox to be logically spoken of? It is this, but It is also that. How is one to speak of such a contradiction? Before long, two separate terms came to be used in order to distinguish that which moves from that which does not, that which is God's Power of creation from God Himself. The unchanging God was often called, *Brahman*; sometimes simply "the Lord." And His mysterious creative Power was called, *Maya*. An explanation of the concept of *Maya* can be found clearly formulated in the *Svetasvatara Upanishad:*

> There is ONE in whose hands is the net of Maya, who rules with His power, who rules all the worlds with His power. [3]
> With Maya, his wondrous power, He made all things, and by Maya the human soul is bound.
> Know therefore that nature is Maya, but that God is the ruler of Maya; and that all beings in our universe are parts of His infinite splendor. [4]

By the time of the *Bhagavad Gita* and the *Puranas* (c. 500 B.C.E.), this terminology was traditional:

> The Lord, though without form and attributes, ... has projected this universe out of His divine Maya. Having brought forth this universe, He dwells within all beings and within all things. Yet He remains unaffected, for He is pure Consciousness. [5]

But it was not until Shankara, the great *acharya* (teacher) of non-dual Vedanta, that the principle of *Maya* was clarified and amplified into a definitive philosophical concept. Shankaracharya is believed by some to have lived in the 7th century C.E.; others say it was in the 9th century. What everyone does agree to, however, is that Shankara was, along with the Buddha and Jesus, one of the most profound thinkers and visionaries who ever lived, whose teachings have continued over the centuries to shape and refine our vision of reality.

Like Jesus, Shankara died in his early thirties, but not before he organized a number of monastic Orders, and wrote a number of works in which he set forth a comprehensive philosophy of Unity -- including comment-aries on the *Upanishads,* the *Brahma Sutras,* and a number of independent treatises, chief among which is *Vivekachudamani,* "The Crest-Jewel Of Discrimination." In this small book, written as a dialogue between a Master and a disciple, he expounds the philosophy of super-imposition based on his own mystical experience.

Having experienced, during meditation, an expansion of his normally limited consciousness, he realized that he was truly the one Consciousness of all, the One who is manifesting as all this universe. He realized this one Supreme Self to be the self of all beings, though they live under the delusion that they are separate individual entities. He realized that there was only this One, that It was unlimited, undivided, eternal and unchanging; that It was the supreme Consciousness which the sages of the *Upanishads* had experienced and called *Brahman.*

Then, returning to the limited awareness of the individual soul, to the world of multiplicity, division and change, he declared that this world is really not different from *Brahman,* but is simply a different perspective, bound by time and space, on the same one Reality. *Brahman* is really pure Consciousness, but somehow -- by a magic known only to Itself -- It manifests as all these forms which collectively we call 'the universe.' "Brahman," says Shankara,

> is the Reality -- the one Existence, absolutely independent of human thought or idea. Though the universe seems to be composed of diverse forms, it is Brahman alone.
> ... No matter what a deluded man may think he is perceiving, he is really seeing Brahman and nothing else

> but Brahman. He sees mother-of-pearl and imagines
> that it is silver. He sees Brahman and imagines that It is
> the universe. But this universe, which is superimposed
> upon Brahman, is nothing but a name. [6]

For Shankara, there is no real duality at all between the
absolute *Brahman* and the world, for the world is not other
than *Brahman*; it is an appearance projected, or
superimposed, upon *Brahman*, as we might superimpose
the mirage of a lake on a stretch of desert sand, or as we
might superimpose an imaginary snake upon a piece of rope
lying in the road. According to him, the mystical vision
reveals that there is but one Existence; the world is not
separate from It, but is simply an appearance of multiplicity
of form where in fact there is only the one Self of pure
Consciousness. Nowadays, we would say that *Brahman*
and the world are 'complementary' perspectives on one
reality, each excluding the other, but both required to
constitute and define the whole.

This projection, says Shankara, of the universe of forms
upon *Brahman* is accomplished by His own Power which is
called, *Maya*:

> Maya is the power of the Lord. She is without
> beginning, ... and is the underlying Cause of all effects. ...
> It is She who brings forth this entire universe. [7]

Note that *Brahman* is genderless, but as "the Lord," He
is referred to as masculine. *Maya* is always regarded as of
the female gender. He is the Father-God; She is the Mother
of all creation. But *Maya* is not only the supreme Power
that generates and animates the universe, She is, at the
same time, that very universe which we perceive. She is at
once the Cause (the creative Power) and the effect (the

phenomenal universe). But, Shankara reminds us, *Maya* (the universe) is only an appearance; the Reality underlying it is *Brahman*; and that is who we really are. All the forms in this world, including man, are the appearances of *Brahman,* Therefore, by understanding and contemplating one's true Identity, says Shankara, one can free oneself from delusion, and experience one's Self as *Brahman.*

Shankara's entire philosophy may be summarized in one of his sayings:

> *brahma satyam*
> *jagat mithya*
> *jivo brahmaiva naparah*

> Brahman is the Reality,
> The world is an [illusory] image;
> The soul [or Self] of man, therefore, is nothing
>   but Brahman.

Shankara teaches that, though our true Identity is concealed from us by *Maya*, we can dispel this ignorance through the practice of discrimination, understanding that we are not the body, the mind, or an individual soul, but are, in fact, the uninvolved, eternal Witness of the mind, body and the soul. By meditating on this truth, he says, we can realize, and become established in, the awareness of *Brahman*, the Supreme Self:

> The Self is the ancient, supreme Being. It never ceases to experience infinite joy. It is always the same. It is Consciousness itself.
> ... It is the knower of the activities of the mind and the individual soul. It is the witness of all the actions of the body, the sense-organs and the vital energy. It

seems to be identified with all of these, ... but It does not act, nor is It subject to the slightest change.

The Self is distinct from Maya, the primal cause, and from her effect, the universe. The nature of the Self is pure Consciousness. ... With a controlled mind and an intellect which is made pure and tranquil, realize the Self within you. Know the Self as the real *I*. Thus will you cross the shoreless ocean of this world, whose waves are birth and death, and live always blessed, in the knowledge of identity with Brahman. [8]

2.   SANKHYA

One can easily imagine the difficulties of explaining the principle of *Maya* satisfactorily, and of defending it against those who choose to ridicule it as a "world-negating" concept. Perhaps for that reason, in another part of India, a different tradition had been formed along the same pattern, but employing different terms to represent the two aspects of reality. It was, in fact, one of the first efforts to put the expression of the duality-in-unity concept into an organized philosophical system, and it was attributed to an ancient sage by the name of Kapila (ca. 900 B.C.E.). His representation of reality came to be known as *Sankhya* ("knowledge" or "wisdom").

Kapila asserted that there was an underlying universal Consciousness that he called *Purusha* (the "Person," the Male principle), which was beyond all qualities and activities, and which was the true *Atman* ("Self") of all beings. And that the aspect of Reality which was perceived as the multiform universe was an undifferentiated creative Energy which he called *Prakrti* (Mother "Nature," the Female principle). Man's ultimate goal, according to Kapila, was to penetrate beneath the surface appearance of *Prakrti*, and realize his true identity as the one *Purusha*, the Self of all.

In that great classic of mystical literature, the *Bhagavad Gita,* written presumably around the same time as the earliest *Puranas* (ca. 500 B.C.E.), Kapila's philosophy found its fullest and most influential expression. In it, Krishna, represented as a manifestation of the Lord, speaks with the voice of the One, to his devotee, Arjuna, and more elaborately explains His dual identity as *Purusha* and *Prakrti*:

> Wherever a being may be born, Arjuna, know that My Prakrti is his Mother, and I [Purusha] am the Father who gave him life. [9]
> ... Prakrti is the source of all material things; it is the creator, the creating, and the creation. Purusha is the Source of consciousness. ... The Purusha in man, united with Praktri, experiences the ever-changing conditions of Prakrti. When he identifies with the ever-changing, he is whirled through life and death to a good or evil fate. But the Purusha in man is ever beyond fate. ... He is the supreme Lord, the supreme Self.
> That man who knows that he is the Purusha, and understands the changing conditions of Prakrti, is never whirled around by fate, wherever he may be. [10]

Purusha is the true Identity of all beings; It is eternal and absolutely free of the transient appearance of the world. Prakriti constitutes all that appears as the world, both the subtle and the gross; but Purusha is the Divine witness, the constant Source and ultimate Ground of all that is.

> .. He who knows that he is, himself, the Lord of all, and is ever the same in all, immortal though experiencing the field of mortality, he knows the truth of existence.
> ... When a man realizes that the Purusha in himself is the same Purusha in all, he does not hurt himself by hurting others. This is the highest knowledge. He who sees that all actions, everywhere, are only the actions of Prakrti, and that the Purusha is the witness of these actions, he sees the truth. [11]
> ... Through My Prakrti, I bring forth all creation, and all these worlds revolve in the cycle of time. But I am not bound by this vast display of creation; I exist alone, watching

the drama of this play. I watch, while Prakrti brings forth all
that moves and moves not; thus the worlds go on revolving.
But the fools of the world know Me not; ... they know not the
supreme Spirit, the infinite God of all.

Still, there are a few great souls who know Me, and who
take refuge in Me. They love Me with a single love, knowing
that I am the Source of all.

They praise Me with devotion; ... their spirit is one with
Me, and they worship Me with their love. They worship Me,
and work for me, surrendering themselves in My vision.
They worship Me as the One and the many, knowing that all
is contained in Me. [12]

So, as we see, the system of Kapila and that of the
Vedanta of the Upanishads and later of Shankara are
philosophically identical, and are differentiated from one
another only by their terminology. Both of these
philosophical systems were born, not of a deliberate
rational attempt to construct a plausible world-view, but
rather of an ineluctible vision, revealed to the mind in the
transcendent experience of unity, though occurring to two
different men at widely separated periods in history. It is a
grave mistake, in my opinion, to view these two
explanations of Reality, as some historians and scholars
tend to do, as mere intellectual constructions to be analyzed
for academic categorization. They are both attempts, on
the part of men who had clearly experienced the unitive
Reality by the grace of God, to share their vision, their
understanding, for the purpose of offering guidance to
sincere aspirants to truth, and should be examined in that
spirit.

3. TAOISM

In China, an equally ancient tradition called Taoism spoke of the two mystically-perceived aspects of Reality as *Tao* and *Teh*. Its greatest spokesman was the vernerable Lao Tze (b. 601 B.C.E.). In his only book, a collection of maxims called the *Tao Teh Ching*, he characterized the absolute, unchanging and eternal aspect as male, and its world-forming energy aspect as female.

Lao had experienced in deep contemplation that pure transcendent Consciousness which is the eternally remote and unchanging absolute Being; he had known too Its outpouring effulgence which is perceived as the creative energy which constitutes the world of form. In himself he had clearly experienced the mystery of creation emanating from the still and constant Source. These two are the same undivided Reality, yet they constitute two paradoxically disimilar aspects of that Reality. In order to speak intelligibly of these two aspects, the unfluctuating Consciousness and Its power of universal manifestation, he characterized Tao, the unchanging Source, as the Father; and Teh, Its incomprehensible power of creative imagery, as the Mother of all:

> Before heaven and earth existed, there was something formless, silent, alone, unchanging, constant and eternal; It could be called 'the Source of the universe.' I do not know Its name, and simply call It *Tao*. [13]
> ... [But] the Tao that can be spoken of is not the absolute Tao [since to speak of It is to make It an

object separate from oneself]. That nameless [Tao] is the Father of heaven and earth; that which may be named [i.e., Teh, which constitutes all that has name and form] is the Mother of all things. [14]

Chuang Tze, who flourished around 290 B.C.E., is no doubt second in importance to Lao Tze as one of the enlightened mystics of the Taoist school. Having experienced the identical mystical revelation several hundred years after his illustrious predecessor, he spoke with an equal authority of the inexplicable Absolute and Its indescribably miraculous power of creation. In the ancient world, the dual-facetedness of Reality was never more clearly expressed than in the writings of these two patriarchs of Taoism. Here is how Chuang Tze describes the Tao:

> That ONE called Tao is subtle, beyond vision, yet latent in It are all forms. It is subtle, beyond vision, yet latent in It are all objects. It is dark and obscure, yet latent in It is the creative Power of life [Teh]. [15]
>
> The visible world is born of the Invisible; the world of forms is born of the Formless. The creative Energy [Teh] is born from Tao, and all life forms are born of this creative Energy; thus all creation evolves into various forms.
>
> ... Life springs into existence without a visible source and is reabsorbed into that Infinite. The world exists in and on the infinite Void [Tao]; how it comes into being, is sustained and once again is dissolved, cannot be seen.
>
> It is fathomless, like the Sea. Wondrously, the cycle of world-manifestation begins again after every

completion. The Tao sustains all creation, but It is
never exhausted. ... That which gives life to all
creation, yet which is, Itself, never drawn upon -- that
is the Tao. [16]

While it is the Father who is the undiminished Source of
all that is, it is the Mother who makes manifest the bounty
of the Father.

That which gave birth to the universe may be
regarded as the Mother of the universe. [17] ... [It is] the
Womb of creation ... called the Mysterious Female; it
is the root of heaven and earth. [18]

All that is, including one's own self as a living, breathing
creature, is born of the Mother, yet partakes of the Father
who is the fountainhead and underlying Identity of all.

The Tao is an empty cup, yet It is inexhaustible;
It is the fathomless Fountainhead of all things. [19]
From the ancient days till now Its manifestation has
never ceased; it is because of this [Teh] that we perceive
the Father of all. It is the manifestation of forms that
reveals to us the Father. [20] The Tao is never the doer, yet
through It everything is done. [21]
The Tao fathers, and the Teh brings everything forth
as the world of form, time, and space. [22]

These two were not to be thought of as separate, independent forces, but are integral, and merely separated in
language in order to give names to the two aspects of the
one unitive Existence.

These two are the same; they are given different
names in order to distinguish between them.
Together, they constitute the Supreme Mystery. [23]

To hold to the Father, the uncreated, while living and
acting within the creation of the Mother was the frequent
advice of both Lao and Chuang, as it is the message of all
mystics of all times and traditions.

He who holds to the Eternal [Tao] while acting in
the transient [Teh] knows the primal Source from
which all things manifest. [24] Therefore, the sage may
travel all day, yet he never leaves his [inner] store of
provisions. [25]   He who remains aware of the Male
[Tao], while living as the Female [Teh], is a guide to
all the people. [26]

To hold to the remembrance of one's eternal Identity in
the midst of the distracting flux of worldly activity, to hold
to the freedom and bliss of one's truly limitless and
unwavering Self despite the seeming contraries in the world
of appearance, was in the estimation of Lao and Chuang
the true legacy of spiritual knowledge and the path to the
blessedness of the wise.

My teaching is very easy to understand and very
easy to practice, yet no one understands it and no one
practices it; [it is this:] the sage wears a tattered coat
[the body of Teh] and carries jade [the treasure of
Tao] within his breast. [27]
[Know that] Teh is your clothing, and Tao is your
sanctuary. [28]

This is just another way of saying that the remembrance of one's real inner treasure, one's eternal identity, lifts one above the petty concerns of one's temporal life amid the hubbub of the world, and bestows calm, clarity, and a sweet joy that can never be defiled. The wise man's remembrance of his eternal identity bestows a security that knows no fear, no distress, in even the most dangerous circumstances, for he

> dwells in the Foundation of the form, and not in the form; he dwells in the fruit, and not in the flowering; thus he holds to the one, and ignores the other. [29]
>
> Therefore, he is not vulnerable to weapons of war; the horns of the buffalo cannot touch him; the claws of the tiger cannot rip him; the sword cannot cut him. Why? Because he is beyond death. [30]

To discover, as Lao and Chuang had discovered, that secret of existence, they advised the quieting of the mind in meditation or contemplation. For this wisdom was inherent in all, and true vision was available to all who would silence the ever-clamoring thoughts that filled the mind with mundane trivia; and peer into themselves as in a rippled pond, awaiting the clear reflection of eternity in the finally calm and serene surface.

> If you want to know the Tao, ... give a bath to your mind; wash your mind clean. Throw out all your sage wisdom! [31]
>
> ... Repose brings good fortune. Without inner repose, your mind will be galloping about, even though you are sitting still. Withdraw your senses within and cease all activity of the mind.

Concentrate your will. Let your ears cease to hear; let your mind cease to imagine. Let your spirit be blank, passively receptive. In such receptivity, the Tao is revealed. [32]

The man of wisdom shuts his senses, closes all doors, dulls his edges, unties all knots, softens his light, calms his turmoil -- this is called attainment of unity with the One. [33]

I guard my awareness of the One, and rest in harmony with externals. ... My light is the light of the Sun and the moon. My life is the life of heaven and earth. Before me is the Undifferentiated [Teh], and behind me is the Unknowable [Tao]. Men may all die, but I endure forever. [34]

4. BUDDHISM

In the 5th century before the Current Era, there lived in India a sage known as "the Buddha," the enlightened one, who initiated yet another mystical tradition. Born into a princely life in the bustling town of Kapilavastu (named for the sage, Kapila), in the kingdom of Koshala, young Siddhartha of the Gautama clan grew up amid wealth and comfort. He married and had a son. But at the age of twenty-nine, he suddenly struck out alone into the forest to enjoy the solitude and peace he felt necessary to the contemplation of truth.

Living alone in a wooded grove beside a river on the outskirts of a small village, Siddhartha gave himself to deep thought, endeavoring to penetrate the mystery of existence. One evening, sitting beneath a sheltering tree, he experienced an unprecedented clarity of mind, and the unity of all life was directly revealed to him. Suddenly, his mind, free of its normal limitations, was the all-inclusive Consciousness of the universe, and all sentient and insentient beings were realized to be manifestations of himself. Never again would he imagine that he was just this one isolated self of Siddhartha; he was the Self of the whole world. Everything was now clear to him; and shortly thereafter he began teaching his message of Enlightenment to others and gathered about him a large following.

In those times, as now, men possessed varying degrees of intelligence and learning, and therefore many different views on the meaning and purpose of life were expounded. The teachings of the *Upanishads* and the Sankhya philosophy were known only to the few and followed by yet fewer. In most cases, even these great philosophies became corrupted by those who had not themselves attained enlightenment. For the most part, men and women followed a less stringent regimen, seeking, as they do today, merely to lead conventional lives of piety and righteousness, giving respect to the holy and alms to the poor. Incapable of sustained contemplation, they worshipped their God through service and priest-led ritual.

The priests who directed the course of these rituals were of the social caste known as *brahmins*, as they supposedly maintained an inner connection with *Brahman* through the repetition of formalized prayers from the *Vedas*, and through the ritualized offerings of sacrifices, or *yajnas*. Thus, the priesthood, supported by the populace, maintained their positions as intermediaries essential to religious worship by teaching a dualistic philosophy based on the separation between man and God (just as priests everywhere have always done) -- a separation which could be breached only by their specialized intercession.

To the Buddha, however, such a religious tradition was puerile and demeaning. He had known the Truth directly, and he knew that only this direct knowledge had the power to satisfy the longing for certainty in every man, and to free the mind from the suffering and sorrow connected with ignorance. And so, to the eager and intelligent young men and women who flocked to hear him, he taught the way of Enlightenment.

It is a fact of religious history that, when the world forgets the true spiritual ideals, and men lose sight of the meaning of life, 'reformers' appear to lead men back to the fundamental and ultimate goal of God-realization. The

Buddha, like all of the greatest of the renowned saints of
every land and every religious tradition -- Shankara, Rumi,
Nanak, St. Francis -- was a 'reformer' in the sense that he
served to recall men to the perennial quest. He was a
mystic, one who had actually realized the Truth of
existence, and who exhorted his brothers to that same
attainment.

The Buddha was not interested in mollifying the weak;
there were enough priests already carrying on that work.
Nor was he interested in further involving aspirants to
Truth in the elaboration of metaphysical doctrines; his
purpose was to enable others to experience what he had,
for he understood clearly that no amount of indoctrination
of metaphysics could take the place of the direct and
immediate experience of Enlightenment, of *nirvana*. For
this reason, he continually exhorted his followers to the
practice of self-introspection and contemplation.

Despite the Buddha's refusal to elaborate a complete
metaphysics, a metaphysics evolved within Buddhism,
nonetheless, just as it must so long as men think and speak.
The One, the ultimate Reality, which the Buddha
experienced came to be called, *Dharmakaya* ("the totality
of Being"). Here, in a Buddhist scripture called the
Avatamsaka Sutra, the *Dharmakaya* is described:

> The Dharrmakaya, though manifesting Itself as the
> three worlds, is free from impurities and desires. ... It is
> forever serene and eternal. It is the One, devoid of all
> determinations. ... There is no place in the universe
> where It does not exist; but though the universe comes
> into being and passes away, the Dharmakaya remains
> forever. Though It is free from all opposites and

contraries, still It works within all beings to lead them to Freedom.[35]

And just as *Brahman* has Its *Maya*, and *Purusha* Its *Prakrti*, *Dharmakaya* also has Its inherent Power of Will which, according to the *Suvarna Prabha*, "creates all the physical bodies and subtle bodies, while the *Dharmakaya*, Itself, does not suffer one whit of change on this account."[36] This Power of physical manifestation is called the *Purvapranidhanabala* ("the primary Power of Will").

So, as I hope the reader is beginning to perceive, the various "religions" and their attendant philosophies, differ from one another only in linguistic terminology. The experience they describe is one, and their intellectual conceptualizations of Reality also are identical, despite the different terminologies adopted over the ages.

5. SHAIVISM

India is a vast and ancient land, and her treasure of seers, sages and yogis is enormous. So it is not surprising that in yet another part of India, another tradition had been developing. It is perhaps the oldest tradition alive today, dating back to pre-Aryan civilization. It is known as *Shaivism*. In this ancient heritage, the aspect of reality which is Absolute and without attributes, the counterpart of *Brahman* and *Purusha*, is *Shiva*. The creative Energy aspect, corresponding to *Maya* and *Prakrti*, is *Shakti*. *Shiva* is a name used for the Lord since prerecorded time. Relics from the ruins of the ancient Dravidian cities of Harappa and Mohenjo-daro indicate that the great god, *Shiva*, was worshipped perhaps as far back as three thousand years before the Current Era.

Shaivism, the worship of Shiva, has no doubt continued uninterrupted from before the arrival of the Aryan intruders up to the present time throughout India. One of its most interesting manifestations, however, occurred around the 8th century C.E., in Kashmir. At that time, a highly refined religious philosophy evolved that became known as *Kashmir Shaivism*.

Though there are a number of philosophical works representing this movement, its main text is a book of maxims of highly concentrated meaning said to be revealed by *Shiva* Himself, called the *Shiva Sutras*. With the intention of avoiding the difficulties of those who held that the universe was an "illusory" product of *Maya*, the philosophers of this school made it very clear that the manifestation of the universe was not an illusion, but was as integral a part of *Shiva* as light was of fire. They reiterated the old truth that the universe is an appearance of *Shiva*, a manifestation of *Shiva's* Power, or *Shakti*. The term, *Shakti*, is of course synonymous with *Prakrti* or *Maya*, and, like those other names, is of the female gender; but it was most carefully and clearly defined so that it would be understood that it was inseparable from Shiva, the Lord, being merely His 'Power of Will,' so that there was no room for the possibility of an illusionist or dualistic interpretation. Here are a few such statements from various sources of the time:

> He knows the true Reality who sees the entire universe as the play of the supreme Shakti of supreme Shiva. [37]

> ... Throughout all these forms, it is the Lord alone; He illumines His own nature. In truth, there is no other cause of all manifestation except His Will (*Shakti*) which gives existence to all worldly enjoyment and liberation as well. [38]

> ... In truth, there is no difference between Uma (*Shakti*) and Shankara (*Shiva*); the One consists of two aspects; of this there is no doubt. [39]

> Shiva and Shakti are not different from each other. Because Shiva contains Shakti, He controls all activities in this multifaceted universe. [40]

> The absolute Consciousness, of Its own free Will, is the cause of the manifestation of the

universe. By the Power [*Shakti*] of Its own free
Will, it unfolds the universe upon Itself. [41]

The entire world is the play of universal
Consciousness. It has become the universe. [42]

In India, therefore, as elsewhere in the world, we find
an astonishing polyglot of traditions intermingling and
confused with one another. But it can be seen that
underneath the apparent diversity is a very simple and
unvarying unanimity; as it is said in the *Rig Veda*: "God is
one; sages call Him by various names." And His Power of
manifestation -- whether we call it *Prakrti, Maya,
Purvapranidhanabala* or *Shakti* -- is also one. The vision
of the seer has never changed, though it has been told and
retold in a million ways, and in countless tongues, since the
beginning of time.

Over the centuries, India has seen the development of
countless expressions of the mystic's vision of reality; and
always we find this recurring pair: the Absolute and the
relative, the eternal One and the temporal manifestation.
And invariably -- in the folk-art and in the poetry of the
people -- these two are portrayed as an inseparable and
complementary couple, as male and female, as Beloved and
lover. Sometimes they are represented in the person of
Narayan (Vishnu) and Lakshmi; in another place they may
be characterized as Krishna and Radha; in yet other men's
eyes they are the mighty Mahadev (Shiva) and his consort,
Parvati (Shakti). Poets and artists make their stories and
their figures to represent these two philosophical
abstractions and thus tell in their own ways the tale of the
mystic's vision. Thus we see, for example, a statue of

Shakti, wild-faced and arms akimbo, dancing on the prone figure of Shiva in a graphic depiction of the relationship between the One who is the unmoving Ground and Foundation of all and His active Power of universal manifestation and destruction. In the verses of the medieval poet-saint, Jnaneshvar, these two lovers are portrayed as "the only ones who dwell in this home called the universe":

> The supreme Reality which is One appears to be two. Through Her, the absolute Void became the primal Person; and She derived Her existence from Her Lord. Shiva formed his beloved of Himself; and without Her presence, no Person exists. ... Because of God, the Goddess exists, and without Her, He is not. They exist only because of each other.
>
> How sweet is their union! The whole world is too small to contain them, yet they live happily in the smallest particle. They regard each other as their own Self, and neither creates so much as a blade of grass without the other. Because of Her, He assumes the form of the universe. Without Her, He is left naked. Although He is manifest, He cannot be seen. It is only by Her grace that He appears as universal form. When He embraces Her, it is His own bliss that Shiva enjoys.
>
> He is the Enjoyer of everything, but there is no enjoyment without Her. She is His form, but Her beauty comes from Him. By their intermingling, they are together enjoying this banquet. [43]

It is a mistake on the part of students of Indian culture to infer from her works of art that India worships primitive gods, just as it would be a mistake on the part of a student of medieval Western civilization to infer from the Cistine Chapel paintings that men of that time and place

worshipped a white-bearded, muscle-bound God who
imparted His spirit to men with a touch of his finger.

Artists and poets have no other media by which to
represent the Formless except form; their portrayals of God
must necessarily be figurative. And so naturally we find a
great abundance of religious symbolism in a culture so
religiously inclined: we find figures of three-headed gods
(representing the three powers of Creation, Sustenance,
and the Destruction of the universe); we find multi-armed
goddesses of Destruction (representing the multi-faceted
reciprocal forces of Nature); and we find the often
misunderstood *lingam* and the *yoni* (the male organ
representative of the transcendent God and the female
organ representative of His creative Power). But let us
understand that the visual and poetic symbols of *Shiva* and
His inseparable Power are symbols only, and point to an
extra-sensual and undivided reality; they are merely
reminders, expressions, of a profound understanding of the
nature of our own Reality.

6. JUDAISM

The Judaic religion was, according to tradition, begun by Abraham, a native of the city of Ur of the Chaldees around 1900 B.C.E. Abraham's trek from his adopted town of Haran well north of Ur southward to the land of Canaan, and the wanderings of his nomad progeny in that area is well documented in the religio-history set down by various hands over the years that followed. The various books recounting the stories of the trials and conquests, exiles and ultimate rulership by the descendants of Abraham over the people indigenous to the land of Canaan were written between the 9th and 6th centuries B.C.E., and gathered, in the 5th century B.C.E., into a collection called the Torah, known to later Christians as the Old Testament of the Bible.

This great collection of books constitutes not only a history of the Jews, but is a testament of their religion as well, beginning with a recounting of the creation of the world by God, whom they called *Yahweh*. However, we must not imagine that these legends of creation were born in some sort of cultural isolation; not at all. They were retellings (or mistellings) of ancient stories gathered from a number of pre-literate indigenous sources. The "prophets" and documentors who wrote the books of the Torah were greatly influenced by the peoples and literature of the land in which they lived. And so there were Sumerian, Babylonian, Akkadian, Egyptian, and Assyrian influences, for there had been a well developed mystically-based religious literature in these regions by the time these books of the Jews were written and collected.

The mystic's vision of an eternal Consciousness at the core of all universal manifestation is the foundation of nearly every early "religious" tradition of which we know. In such "vision," one experiences the Eternal Source as transcendent and unchanging; the manifested universe is seen as an effulgence emanating from that unchanging Consciousness as a kind of Thought-Energy which takes form as the world. These two aspects of the one Reality appear in nearly every early mythology and religious system which has come down to us.

In the religious literature of Egypt (c. 2500 B.C.E.), for example, a rich literary heritage centered around the God of the Memphites, called *Ptah*, and His creative Thought or Word, called *Atum*, by which all that is was created. To his followers, *Ptah* was the one unchanging Source; His Thought produced all creation. In upper Egypt, the one God was known by the name, *Neter*, and at other times, *Amon-Re*; and the proliferation of names and qualities, over the years, produces for us today the impression of a polytheistic pantheon of separate figures.

In nearly every historical instance, the transcendent, unmanifest Father-God is thought of as male, and His power of creative Thought which gives expression or utterance to the whole universe of temporal forms is thought of as the female element, the Mother of all creation. Like a human mind and its power of thought, these two are integral complements -- a One with two different aspects of being; one unchanging, eternal; the other fomenting constant temporal change.

In the ancient Near-East, from Egypt to Sumer to Babylon and Canaan, there was a widespread recognition of these two complementary aspects of the one Divine

Reality, personified as male and female, as they have been recognized and personified in myth and allegory in nearly every culture from time immemorial. The names given to these personalized forms of the two complementary principles were many: for the Sumerians, they were *An* and *Inanna*. In Babylon, they were *Apsu* and *Tiamat*. In the land of Canaan, where many different cultural strains met and intermingled, they were *El* and *Athirat* (or *Asherah*), or they were *Ba'al* and *Ba'ala*. It must be remembered, however, that, for the mystic, the seer, these two are never separate from one another, but are complementary aspects of the one Reality.

During Biblical times (1900-900 B.C.E.), the tribes of Jews who came to live in this stretch of land called Canaan found this mystical religion of duality-in-Unity offensive and promulgated their own religious philosophy based primarily on their belief in their special favor in the eyes of their own personalized tribal God. It therefore became a vested interest of the religious leaders of the Jews to propagandize the theology of the Canaanites as a primitive dualism or even polytheism, and to warn their followers against tolerating the religion of the Canaanites.

In several books of the Old Testament, the anathema against worshipping in the manner of the Canaanites is repeated both implicitly and explicitly. Those found using the image of the bull calf (symbol of the Ba'al, or Male, complement of Divinity) or the ash tree or column (symbolic of the Asherah, or Female, aspect) in their worship were condemned and persecuted.

Nonetheless, the deeply ingrained cultural influences of this mystically-based religious tradition rubbed off on the more broad-minded of the Jews; and they adopted the

concept of a creative Mother-power emanating from
Yahweh, their Father-God, which they called *Chokmah*, or
"Wisdom." She is referred to in the Biblical book of
Ecclesiasticus as "the Word that was spoken by the Most
High," from which all the universe is formed:

> *Chokmah* is from the Lord; She is with Him
> eternally. ... It is He who created Her, ... and infused
> Her into all His works. [44]

> Before God made the earth and the fields or the
> first dust of the world, when He set up the heavens, I
> [Chokmah] was there; ... When He laid the found-
> ations of the earth, I existed as His instrument." [45]

We find this same esoteric concept carried over in the book
of *Genesis*, as God speaks the Word and so it comes to be:
"God said, 'Let there be light,' and there was light."

And so, while we can find in the Judaic scriptures traces
of an original myth of a Divine Consciousness which
projects Itself, through Its power of Thought, as a world of
living creatures and objects, that myth had undergone a
major transformation by the time it reappeared in the
Jewish Patriarch's retelling of Creation in the major portion
of the book of *Genesis*. Instead of an all-inclusive *ONE*, in
whose very being the world exists, and from whom the
world and its creatures can never be separated, the One
had become a separate being, a god, standing apart from
His creatures as a vengeful and tyrannical overlord. This is
a wonderful example of the sad but perennial corruption of
the teachings of the mystic seers by the uninitiated which

results in the objectification of Deity as an entity separate from one's own identity and from all phenomenal reality.

Such a dualistic view of reality is a failure of vision which results in a narrow and self-alienating view of life. And yet it is this very view, this mistaken version of the nature of reality, that has influenced the culture of Western civilization so greatly for the last 2000 years that it can no longer be ignored, and must finally be denounced as the false doctrine that it is.

And while it is indeed true that many born into the Judaic religious tradition have been graced, through their ardent devotion to God, with the realization of the great Unity; they have invariably become, by virtue of this very realization, exiled and excluded from that tradition. For to experience and declare one's unity with God gives the lie to the Biblical mythology, and contradicts the Judaic doctrine of the eternal separation of God and His Creation, and the distinction between God and the eternal soul of man.

In the 6th century B.C.E., not far from the land of the Jews, Heraclitus of Ephesus (540-480 B.C.E.) introduced his own mystically-inspired concept of duality-in-unity, attributing to God (*Zeus*) the power of Thought or Ideation (*Logos*) by which He, the unmanifested Absolute, created and governed the motion of all things. This term, *Logos*, was then adopted by the early Stoics, who likewise meant by it the creative Will or Power of manifestation which flowed from the Divine, and which constituted the phenomenal universe.

The philosophy of the *Logos* then reached its ultimate expression in the writings of an Alexandrian Jew, Philo Judaeus (20 B.C.E. to 40 C.E.), a contemporary of Jesus of Nazareth. Like Jesus, Philo was a mystic who alienated himself from the Judaic tradition into which he was born by speaking of his experience of Unity. He attempted in his writings to reconcile Judaism with the mystical philosophy of the Greeks by declaring that the *Logos* was synonymous with the Biblical term, *Chokmah*, characterizing the *Logos* as "the first begotten of God." "The *Logos*," he explained, "was conceived in God's mind before all things and is that which manifests as all things." [46]

Philo was a wealthy, aristocratic statesman and scholar; Jesus was a poor rustic. Philo never heard of Jesus, and Jesus never read Philo. Nonetheless, their vision was essentially the same.

7. CHRISTIANITY

Jesus was a Jew, born in Judea, and raised to manhood in Galilee during the time of the Roman occupation. As a child, he was steeped in the ancient lore of the Jews, and he showed an acute interest in philosophy and religion from the time of his early youth. Around the age of twenty-nine (when Saturn returns to its natal position), Jesus met a teacher called John the Baptist, who served to initiate the process of his awakening to the Divinity within him.

Jesus then spent some time in solitude, praying to the God whom he addressed as his "Father"; and one night, in the intensely focused concentration of his prayer and longing, his mind was lifted into a pure silence by which it became absolutely clear. In that clarity, in that silence, he transcended his own individuality and entered into a realm of awareness (the Kingdom of God) heretofore unknown to him, wherein he experienced the clear realization that he and the Father were one -- that the one Consciousness of the universe was who he really was. His mind became merged in the universal Mind, and he knew the star-filled cosmos as his own radiating effulgence.

For some time he marvelled at the infinite glory of his newfound Self, a Self whom he had always been, but had heretofore been blind to. He who had, moments before, wept in longing for his heavenly Father's embrace, now bathed in the knowledge that He himself was the one and only ocean of bliss and source of all that was. It was a profound and lasting revelation, one that overwhelmed all previous notions of a separate, individual identity.

Jesus continued in solitude for some time, reflecting on this new knowledge, and searching his thoughts for some indication of what he was to do with it. Other possibilities presented themselves, but he knew in his heart that he had no choice but to spend his life glorifying among men the One who had so graciously revealed Himself. Such knowledge could not be withheld; it had to be shared with everyone. It was the knowledge that would release men from their mistaken ideas of the world, of their bewilderment and despair, and herald a New Age of joy. It appeared to him that it was he, Jesus of Nazareth, who was called upon to be the "Anointed one" whom the ancient prophets of the Jews had spoken of in their predictions. And so Jesus returned to his friends to share his "good news," to tell others of what had been revealed in him.

Jesus recognized in the Psalms of David a lineage of fervent devotion to God, a lineage to which he himself belonged; and he sought only to attest to and reaffirm that eternal religion of Love -- the inner purification of the heart which alone leads to the clear vision of God. This inner vision Jesus spoke of as an entering into "the kingdom of God." But the orthodox rabbis and religious leaders, unaware of the fact of mystical experience, did not believe that God could be "seen" or known; nor did they believe that they themselves were manifestations of God. Such ideas went beyond their comprehension, and so were labeled heretical.

The religious leaders of the Jewish community therefore accused Jesus to his face of portraying God contrary to the traditions of Judaism, and he answered to them: "You say that He is your God, yet you have not known Him; but I have known Him." [47] And he attempted to explain to them that the Consciousness within them, the Self which knows itself as "I AM," is the eternal God, the everlasting Self of the universe, who could be realized, as he had done, through fervent devotion and contemplation.

But the council of elders and high priests were convinced that to allow the teaching that man is God in essence would undermine all morality, and corrupt the youth by inviting them to claim that all their acts were the acts of God. And so they voted to condemn Jesus as a heretic, and they plotted to turn him over to the Roman authorities as a criminal against the state. Thus, when Jesus came to the city of Jerusalem during the celebration of the Jewish holiday called Passover, he was arrested, tried, and condemned to death by the high priests. He was then turned over to the Romans and cruelly executed by them.

The tragedy of Jesus was that of a great lover of God who had realized the highest knowledge and tried to share it, but was not understood by his own people, and was slain by them. But his tragedy served to uplift the consciousness of the world, for today he is remembered and honored everywhere as an inspiration to all people who would know God by the path of love and who would manifest His Love in their very lives.

Jesus never adopted the concept of the *Logos*, nor did he ever write out a concisely formulated metaphysics; but though he often referred to the distinction between the absolute Consciousness and the world of matter as a duality of the Spirit and the flesh, or of "the Father" and "the son," it is clear that he never regarded this duality as absolute and

irresolvable; rather, he saw the flesh as a manifestation of
the spirit, the "son" as a manifestation of the "Father":

> If you knew who I am, you would also know the
> Father. Knowing me, you know Him; seeing me, you see
> Him. ... Do you not understand that I am in the Father
> and the Father is in me? ... It is the Father who dwells
> in me doing His own work. Understand me when I say
> that I am in the Father and the Father is in me. [48]

Although the concept of the *Logos* -- a creative Energy
projected from and upon the universal Consciousness and
manifesting as universal form -- was never recorded as a
part of Jesus' teaching, it is clear that had he known of the
term, he would have acknowledged its validity. The author
of the Fourth Gospel of the New Testament, who lived
about a hundred years after Jesus, and who is known to us
only as John, *was* familiar with the term, however, and was
most likely well versed in the writings of Philo. He adopted
the Greek word, *Logos*, in place of the Hebrew word,
Chokmah, and began his recounting of the life of Jesus
with these famous words:

> In the beginning was the *Logos* [often translated as
> "Word"]; the *Logos* was with God, and the *Logos* was
> [conceptually separate from, but essentially identical
> with] God.
> ... All things were made by the *Logos*; without him
> nothing was made. It was by him that all things came
> into existence. [49]

John, following Philo's characterization of the
Chokmah/Logos as "the only begotten of God," refers to the
Logos as "him" (despite the traditional characterization of

Chokmah/Logos as feminine), and went on to assert that the *Logos* had "become flesh" only in the person of Jesus, thus limiting and distorting the original meaning of the term. For, originally, for Heraclitus and Philo, as well as for the author of *Ecclesiasticus*, *Chokmah/Logos* represented the universal creative Energy which "became flesh" in the person of each and every creature in the cosmos.

Later, in the 2nd century C.E., during the years of struggle to formulate a viable set of doctrines for a disorganized Church, Clement of Alexandria, Justin Martyr, and other Christian apologists vehemently defended the Johanine idea that the *Logos* became flesh uniquely and exclusively in the person of Jesus of Nazareth; and thereafter, the *Logos* became popularly regarded as a term synonymous with Jesus, "the only begotten son of God." Since that time, the *Logos* has so often been associated with this idea, that it has lost much of its original meaning.

8. ISLAM

Islam, founded in the 7th century C.E. by Muhammed, is, like Christianity, a monotheistic religious tradition that, while being the teaching of one man, has its primary theological base in the more ancient Judaic scriptures. And, like Judaism and Christianity, its official philosophy is dualistic; that is, it holds that God and His creation are forever separate and distinct. Nonetheless, as in Judaism and Christianity, there have been occasional mystics within Islam who have not only realized but proclaimed that God, the soul and the world are ultimately one; and, as in Judaism and Christianity, they have always been regarded by the orthodox of their own tradition as blasphemers and heretics. Thus, it is the common shame of these three traditions that the greatest of their followers, the most blessed of their seers -- their Spinozas, their Eckharts, their al-Hallaj's -- are invariably maligned and persecuted as heretics.

Within Islam, those seers who represent the mystic strain are called "Sufis,"a term which refers to the cotton garments worn by the early mystics of Islam. And in the early centuries of Islam many of these Sufis confounded the orthodox by speaking boldly of their experience of the identity of the soul and God. Abu Yazid al-Bastami (d. 875 C.E.) cried out, "Praise be to me!" Mansur al-Hallaj (d. 922 C.E.) uttered the famous "*an al-Haqq*" ("I am the Truth"), and added, "I am He whom I love and He whom I love is I. We are two dwelling in one body. If you see me, you see Him, and if you see Him, you see us both." [50]

But a clear and concise philosophy of unity was not formulated until the appearance of the gifted Muhyid-din Ibn al-Arabi, known in the West simply as Ibn Arabi. Born in Spain in 1165 C.E., Ibn Arabi was a contemporary of Saint Francis of Assisi (1182-1224), and of two other famous mystic-poets of the Sufi tradition: the Persian, Jalal-ud-din Rumi (d. 1273), and the Turk, Farid-ud-din Attar (d. 1230). Ibn Arabi held a view identical to all others who have clearly "seen" the unity; he maintained that the One and the many, the universal Consciousness and the phenomenal universe, are simply two perspectives on the same one Reality.

The terms Ibn Arabi employed to distinguish these two perspectives, or aspects, of Reality are *Haqq* and *Khalq*. When we experience the unmanifest One (in the transcendent state of consciousness), we are experiencing *Haqq*; when we experience the world of multiple phenomena (through our individual senses), we are experiencing *Khalq*. "But," says Ibn Arabi, "the *Haqq* of whom transcendence is asserted is the same as the *Khalq* of whom immanence is asserted, although the one is distinguishable from the other." [51] Thus, Ibn Arabi's vision and his doctrine, like that of the other great mystics of all religious traditions is one of complementarity.

For him, the world (*Khalq*) is simply the appearance of God (*Haqq*). It is simply our limited perspective as individual perceiving entities that produces the appearance of multiplicity. "Multiplicity," he says, "is simply due to the existence of [multiple subjective entities having] different points of view, not to an actual division in the one Essence." [52]   And Unity simply means that, "two or more things are *actually* identical but *conceptually* distinguishable the one from the other; so in one sense the one *is* the other, while in another sense it is not." [53]

> If you regard Him through Him [i.e., while one with Him in the mystical experience of unity], then He regards Himself through Himself; but if you regard Him through yourself [i.e., at the phenomenal level, through the senses], then the unity vanishes. [54]
>
> ... If you assert that only *Haqq* [the Transcendent] is real, you limit God. And if you assert that only *Khalq* [the immanent] is real, you deny Him. But if you assert that both things are real, you follow the right course, and you are a leader and a master in knowledge. [55]

Here, Ibn Arabi describes how, when the mystical vision of unity dawns, it is seen that the One alone exists -- and that It *is* the many:

> When the mystery -- of realizing that the soul is one with the Divine is revealed to you, you will understand that you are no other than God. ... Then you will see all your actions to be His actions and all your attributes to be His attributes and your essence to be His essence.
>
> ... Thus, instead of his own essence, there is the essence of God and in place of his own qualities, there are the attributes of God. He who knows himself sees his whole existence to be the Divine existence, but does not experience that any change has taken place in his own nature [consisting] of qualities. For when you know yourself, your sense of a limited identity vanishes, and you know that you and God are one and the same. [56]
>
> ... There is no existence save His existence. ... This means that the existence of the beggar is His existence, and the existence of the sick is His existence. Now, when this is admitted, it is acknowledged that all existence is His existence; and that the existence of all

created things, both activities and essences, is His existence; and when the secret of one particle of the atoms is clear, the secret of all created things, both outward and inward, is clear, and you do not see in this world or the next, anything except God. [57]

Though Ibn Arabi was never appreciated or accepted by the legalists of Islam in his own time or later, still his writings survived and had great influence upon the more daring of medieval thinkers -- within Islam and Christianity as well.

Another mystic of Islam who deserves mention was Dārā Shikōh (1615-1659), a great-grandson of Akbar, the great Mughal king of India. Dārā Shikōh was tried and executed as a heretic by the fanatic Muslim king, Aurangzeb, for having realized and proclaimed the great unity underlying all existence, and for teaching that the scriptures of India, the *Upanishads,* also taught the true knowledge of God. In his book, *Risāla-yi-Haqq-Numā,* he speaks of his vision of Truth in terms familiar to all who have seen It:

Here is the secret of unity; O friend, understand it:
Nowhere exists anything but God.
All that you see or know other than Him,
Though separate in name, is truly one in essence
with God.

Like an ocean is the essence of the supreme Self;
Like forms in water are all souls and all objects.
The ocean heaving and stirring within,
Transforms itself into drops, waves and bubbles.

So long as it does not realize its unity with the
ocean,

The drop remains a drop;
So long as he does not know himself to be the
    Creator,
The created remains a created.

O you, in quest of God, you seek Him everywhere;
But, truly, you yourself are God, and not apart from
    Him!
Since you are already in the midst of the boundless
    ocean,
Your quest is like that of a drop searching for the
    ocean. [58]

∞   ∞   ∞

PART THREE:

The Knowledge Of The Self

"Frequently consider the connection of all things in the universe.

... Whatever may happen to thee, it was prepared for thee from all eternity; and the progression of causes was from eternity spinning the thread of thy being."

-- Marcus Aurelius,
Commentaries

1.   SCIENCE AND GNOSIS

Throughout history, men have used various words for "knowledge." But there are, in fact, two different *kinds* of knowledge: there is the direct knowledge of the Self, the subjective reality, which we call *gnosis*; and there is the knowledge of nature, the objective reality, which we call *science*. Each kind of knowledge has its own methodology -- and its own limitations. Either kind of knowledge alone without the balance of its counterpart is extremely lopsided and liable to error. The quest for either kind of knowledge to the exclusion of the other is to focus on only half of the equation. "Science without religion [*gnosis*] is lame," said Albert Einstein; "religion without science is blind."

For a long time now, the civilizations of the world have recognized only science as knowledge. No doubt this has occurred as a reaction to the horrors and excesses of blind faith in the utterances of those claiming gnosis without benefit of reason or perceptible evidence. And now, the horrors of a science founded on reason and perceptible evidence alone, crippled by a lack of the sense of Divinity, are all too apparent as well. Hoping to understand Reality solely through empirical, scientific study, we have groped and stumbled along, blundering often in the wrong direction; and finally we have come to see by our long efforts that what those mystics whom we regarded as dreamy fools had been telling us from the beginning is in fact the case.

Acknowledging this, the well-known astronomer and author, Robert Jastrow, states that,

> For the scientist who has lived by his faith in reason,
> the story ends like a bad dream. He has scaled the
> mountains of ignorance; he is about to conquer the
> highest peak; and, as he pulls himself over the final
> rock, he is greeted by a band of theologians who have
> been sitting there for centuries. [1]

In short, the descriptions of the universe by modern physicists are sounding increasingly like the metaphysics expounded by Eastern mystics from the beginning of time. Let me, then, recapitulate the metaphysics of mysticism, so we can compare it with the world-view of modern physicists:

The mystics of both East and West hold that the universe is a manifestation of an insubstantial, yet intelligent creative Energy which, manifesting as form, constitutes the entire phenomenal universe. This Energy (called *Maya* or *Shakti* by the yogis) has no independent existence of its own, but is merely a projection upon a static background of pure Consciousness (whom the yogis call *Brahman* or *Shiva*) -- in much the same way as the thought-energy that constitutes mental-images is a projection of and upon the consciousness of an individual mind.

Thus, the transcendent and absolute Consciousness and the Energy which manifests as the immanent world, are simply complementary aspects of the same one supreme Existence -- just as the water of the ocean and the waves on the ocean are complementary aspects of the ocean. The duality created by dividing Energy from Consciousness is therefore clearly an artificial one, for they constitute an indivisible whole. Nonetheless, the recognition of the apparent duality within the whole is useful, for it reveals the mechanics of the subject-object and the mind-body relationships, which otherwise would be inexplicable.

The one universal Consciousness underlies all existence, not only on the universal level, but on the human level as well. It is the supreme Intelligence of the universe, and it is also the light of awareness in man. It is this underlying Consciousness which gives life to the mind and body. The body itself -- including the brain, nervous system, and all bodily functions -- is a manifestation, as the entire universe is, of the infinitely creative Energy inherent in the absolute Consciousness. Thus appears a duality of mind and body, of subject and object; but this duality is *apparent* only, because they are ultimately undivided, constituting an unbroken Whole.

This 'Eastern metaphysic' which I've just described represents a vision increasingly shared by Western science. And the discoveries of 20th century science, won with such dilligence and dedication to the empirical method, continue to gather inexorably toward a universal world-view which clearly reiterates and confirms the model propounded by the mystical sages and yogis of thousands of years ago. Let us see how the scientific community has come to share with the mystics this vision of the world as an embodiment of Energy:

In the late 19th century, matter had been found to be divisible into molecules; then, molecules were found to be made of still smaller particles, called atoms; then, the atoms were found to be constituted of yet smaller (sub-atomic) particles, such as protons and electrons, which fall into broad categories of hadrons and leptons. Today, physicists theorize that these in turn are composed of a yet tinier entity called quarks, which come in various "flavors": *up, down, strange, charm, top,* and *bottom.* These *quarks, electrons, photons,* and so forth, are names given to actual phenomena perceived, but, we have to ask ourselves, what are all *these* things made of?

Physicists, attempting to answer this question, and to explain the apparently spontaneous creation of all these so-called "elementary particles," have theorized that these particles have no real substance as entities at all, but are mere concentrations of energy arising from a single invisible energy-field. According to this theory, called the Quantum Field Theory, the *Field* is seen as the fundamental reality of all phenomena, and the particles are merely local condensations forming and dissolving within the Field. As Albert Einstein noted,

> There is no place in this new kind of physics both for the field and matter, for the field is the only reality. [2]

But what is this "unified field" from which all of creation supposedly proceeds? How are we to envisualize it? We cannot; for it is again our old friend, *the Invisible Substratum,* with a new name: an all-pervading, intangible and untraceable something, like nothing so much as a universal Mind which projects thought-forms upon its own screen. We may call it, "a field," a "creative Void," or, borrowing a term which has been used for over forty centuries to designate this universal source of phenomena, we may call it, *Shiva,* and name its power of manifesting as form, *Shakti.*

From one viewpoint, the universe is immensely complex. From another viewpoint, it is immensely simple.

It depends on whether you are looking at the ocean or at the waves. From the "simple" viewpoint, the various forms that matter takes is not the answer to what matter is made of; matter is simply made of the *Field* (*Shiva*), in various degrees and permutations of vibratory excitation (*Shakti*), producing the illusion of form. These "illusions" may appear as variously flavored quarks, nuclei, atoms, molecules or complete elephants or supernova; but no matter how intricately woven, the fabric of reality consists ultimately of a single continuum of potentiality which continually manifests and dissolves all these forms upon itself.

The investigations of physicists of the 20th century into the behavior of subatomic particles have led to revolutionary developments in all branches of science, medicine, and industry, enabling us to better understand the life-process and resulting in the saving of lives and in new means of power and communication. These scientists, with their cyclotrons and linear accelerators, have contributed immensely to the accumulation of knowledge of how the various elementary particles behave. But as to what these particles themselves are made of -- we already knew that: they're made of *Shakti*, the vibratory Energy of manifestation inherent in the universal Mind-continuum called *Shiva*.

Now let's see how some of today's scientists have come to recognize, as the mystics have been contending all along, that all things in the universe do indeed "move together of one accord.":

One of the primary assumptions of science is the relationship between cause and effect. Most of what passes as scientific research is an enquiry into local causes. What causes cancer? What causes black holes? What causes poverty? And so on. Generally, we settle arbitrarily on a preceding event or state which we designate as "the cause" of the present state. But scientists are realizing that the web of relationships is endless. Investigations into the nature of sub-atomic events has led them to acknowledge that events are not caused by other isolated events, but are rather linked in a complex web of relationships within a larger common Whole whose nature determines the nature of those constituent events.

In other words, the primary reality is no longer thought to be the independent bits of which the Whole is constituted, but rather the other way around: the primary reality is the Whole, the condition of which governs the functions and interrelations of all constituent parts within the Whole. The logical conclusion is that all local causes must be referred to the condition of the Whole, which must in turn be regarded as the only actual *cause*.

Thus, in the newly emerging wholistic world-view of modern science, the fundamental reality is *the unbroken Whole*. A remarkably lucid statement of this view which warrants appearing here in full is this from a 1975 article written by two respected theoretical physicists, David Bohm and Basil Hiley. According to them, the world which we perceive

> cannot properly be analyzed into independently existent parts with fixed and determinate dynamical relationships between each of the parts. Rather, the "parts" are seen to be in immediate connection, in which their dynamical relationships depend, in an irreducible way, on the state of *the whole system* (and indeed on that of broader systems in which they are contained, extending ultimately and in principle to the entire universe). Thus, one

> is led to a new notion of *unbroken wholeness* which denies the classical idea of analyzability of the world into separately and independently existent parts. We have reversed the usual classical notion that the independent "elementary parts" of the world are the fundamental reality, and that the various systems are merely particular contingent forms and arrangements of these parts. Rather, we say that inseparable quantum interconnectedness of the whole universe is the fundamental reality, and that relatively independently behaving parts are merely particular and contingent forms within this whole. [3]

What this means is that local causes do not exist in any real sense, since all relationships are contingent on the condition of the Whole, and cannot be isolated from the context of the Whole.

Imagine a rolling wave on the ocean: does not each molecule of water in that wave move in a place governed by, and interrelated with, the placement and movement of every other molecule? Are not each of the molecules of water forming that wave all moving "together of one accord?" Now, expand that illustration to include all the molecules of the universe. Are they not all rolling together interrelatedly and of one concerted accord? Is not the universe like one ocean, and the galaxies but eddies in that ocean? Where, then, in the midst of all this motion and expanse can one point to small-scale local causes between entities? Certainly there are countless interactions and relationships, but there is only one impetus, or cause, at the source of and governing all motion and all relationships.

If we must speak of *causes* at all, we must speak of the original Cause as the *only* cause, since the Initiator of the world-drama must be accounted responsible for all that followed the primary creative impulse. Imagine, for example, a number of balls on a billiard table. Each of the balls ricochets off the other in various directions, and one ball falls into the pocket. What caused the ball to go into the pocket? The last ball that hit it, of course. But what caused *that* ball to be rolling in that direction with just that amount of force? Why, the ball that hit *it*. And what caused *that* ball ... etc. As you can see, by the process of regression of causes, we must eventually come to the initial strike of the cue ball by the cue stick. That, we say, was the primary cause of the ball's falling into a pocket.

Extending the regression of causes *ad infinitum* will bring us eventually to the one primary Cause from which all subsequent causes were produced, and in relation to which they all become effects. This "Initiator" has been called "the Divine Will," "the Unmoved Mover," "Maya," "Shakti," and many more names. Whatever we call It, It is responsible for everything that occurs in this universe. It is the one Cause of all that has followed in an inconceivably complex chain of interrelationships. Not a single sparrow's fall, or tumbling of a grain of sand, occurs external to the universal order of unicausal progression.

While it is no doubt true that the world of sub-atomic wave/particles does not follow such clear-cut trajectories as billiard balls, and that the causal progression of their motions is entirely untraceable; nonetheless, the law of unicausality is never broken. There is, shall we say, an interlocking agreement, a perfect accord, in the working of the world, with no possibility of anything at all occurring out of order with the rest. And yet this order is not mechanical; it is more like the growth of a living entity.

Just as the growth of a tulip, filmed in time-lapse sequence, shows the beautiful, coordinated unfoldment of the whole plant to its glorious flowering, and subsequent demise, so does the unfolding universe display just such perfect organic coordination in its every detail. The point I wish to make is that, in the unfolding of the universe, there are no small-scale *causes*; and yet there is an infallible causality at work -- as infallibly sure and definite in its working as in the unfolding of the tulip plant. For there is one primary Cause, and the universe following the unswerving laws of motion and causality, is its effect.

For the mystic, to whom this interconnectedness of the universe has been revealed, it is a matter of absolute certainty. This truth is not demonstrable, however, and therefore is not knowable by the empirical methods of science. It can only be known through *gnosis.*

Let us understand this issue clearly; it is important to distinguish between *science* and *gnosis,* and to understand the capabilities and limitations of each: Empirical science is incapable of demonstrating causes; its only business is and has always been simply to describe the behavior patterns of phenomena. For though science is capable of describing the phenomena of motion, inertia, gravity, mass, space, energy, etc., it has never been able to determine the cause of these phenomena, as science is precluded in principle from the realm of the invisible, undemonstrable source of all phenomena, the *Cause* of the manifestation of phenomena. For the determination of the *Cause*, science must defer to the seers, the mystics. The role of science is then to show whether or not the statements of the seers are consistent with demonstrable evidence.

In the mystic's "vision," the entire universe is seen to be a "projection" of the one absolute Consciousness, that pure Consciousness being the sole Cause and Source of all that is manifest. The manifested universe itself is seen to be of the nature of "thought," having no independent existence of its own. It is sometimes referred to by seers and mystics as "dream-like" or "illusory" in that it is a substanceless fluctuating image whose underlying reality is that eternal Consciousness which produced it. From the mystic's perspective, there is not the slightest doubt that any attempt to discover the ultimate Cause of phenomena by observing the behavior of phenomena is doomed to failure, as the Cause is utterly beyond the reach of sense-perception, being the substratum of both phenomena and perception.

David Bohm, in his book, *Wholeness And The Implicate Order,* attempted to give scientific credence to this mystical world-view, and succeeded in calling world-wide attention to the possibility that such a description is consistent with empirical evidence in general and with Quantum Theory in particular. Indulging his metaphysical bent, he postulated, as a means of preserving the principle of causality, a hidden undemonstrable Source for the manifestation of universal phenomena. He posits, as a sub-reality to the *explicate* order -- i.e., the unfolded, or manifested, world of quantum-based phenomena, an *implicate* or enfolded order of reality which gives rise to the explicate order. Again, it is like nothing so much as the familiar concept of the transcendent, unqualified Source underlying all phenomena that is usually referred to by mystics as "the Divine Mind" or "God."

Bohm, one of the greatest scientists of the twentieth century, has admirably shown that empirical evidence and present scientific theory are not inconsistent with the mystic's vision, and that a viable scientific world-view *is* compatible with the world-view of the mystics. This, truly, is as much as empirical science can hope to achieve. By giving 'God' and 'the world' the new labels of 'implicate order' and 'explicate order,' Bohm offers us yet another pair of terms to signify the absolute and relative aspects of reality. But such verbal re-labeling does nothing, unfortunately, to inform us regarding the hidden Source, and is totally useless as a means to the actual *realization* of the true nature of reality. For, ultimately, reality is not subject to realization by means of concept formulation or verbal explication, but only by *direct* experience; i.e., *gnosis.*

One may certainly *infer* the existence of a transcendent Cause from observing phenomena, and call It 'the implicate order,' but that implicate order is still not subject to empirical proof; i.e., to *scientific* knowledge. The only kind of certain knowledge to which It is subject is the knowledge obtained through intensely focused introspection, as It constitutes the very consciousness existing within every human being, and may only be known as Identity. This kind of direct knowledge is called *gnosis.*

The knowledge of the mystics, which we call *gnosis,* is subjective and undemonstrable, but it is knowledge nonetheless. *Gnosis* is not simply a designation for any and every kind of subjective knowledge; it refers only to the direct form-transcending knowledge of universal Identity, the knowledge of the Absolute, the Godhead. Historically, this knowledge has been relegated to the category of

'religion,' and equated with 'belief.' Yet it is, and should be
re-established as, the summit of human knowledge, and the
guiding light for science.

Science and gnosis do not contradict each other; they
are complementary means of knowledge appropriate to a
Reality which consists of two contrary but complementary
aspects. Gnosis looks to the realm of Consciousness, while
science looks to the realm of phenomena; yet *both*, as
complementary viewpoints, are absolutely necessary to the
whole and complete knowledge of Reality. Indeed, it is the
omission of either one of these complementary viewpoints
that so often gives rise to misunderstanding and error.

2. CONSCIOUSNESS

In the Shaivite text, the *Shiva Sutras*, the very first Sutra states: *Chaitanyam atma;* "The Self is Consciousness." This is a knowledge that is attained, not through science, but through gnosis. To the mystic who has known the unitive Truth, the one all-pervading Consciousness is the sole identity of everyone and everything in the universe; It is, without doubt, the ultimate Source and primary Reality from which the universe of form is projected. There is a movement among modern scientists, however, to view human consciousness as a by-product of evolution, as simply an "effect" of the complex organization of matter. To the mystic, this view is absurd. It is like saying that a dreamer is the *effect* of a sufficiently complex dream, or that the thinker is the effect of a sufficiently complex thought. In order to clarify our understanding on this issue, let us examine for a moment the meaning of consciousness.

Consciousness is not easy for our minds to grasp, because we are It. It is closer than our jugular veins. It is the background of knowing, experiencing, being; it is the life that we regard as self. Consciousness can only be approached subjectively; what we know about it we know from introspection. From the standpoint of the Vedantic sages,

The infinite, all-pervasive, all supporting Brahman
(universal Consciousness) manifests Himself as the *I* in

man. He is the immutable *witness* of the functions of
the intellect in this body. [4]

I am is an immediately evident fact -- perhaps the most
evident of all facts. It is not necessary to think in order to
be aware *I am* -- Descartes' assertion to the contrary
notwithstanding. *I am* is self-evident and logically prior to
thought, for it is the *I* of *I think*. This *I am* (Sanskrit:
Aham; Hebrew: *Ehyeh*) is synonymous with consciousness
in man. It is the constant underlying background which
serves as witness as well as substratum to all possible
mental states.

Just as the terms, "Consciousness" and "matter"
represent the apparent division of the One at the cosmic
level, the same terms, "consciousness" and "matter" (or
"mind" and "body") represent the same duality on the
microcosmic, human, level. Consciousness is the immutable, static witness; what it witnesses is its own projection
in the form of thoughts, feelings, and images, as well as the
impressions registered by the senses. Consciousness is the
subject, the *seer*, and everything else is the object, the
seen.

Consciousness never vanishes; it is the one unfailing
constant witness to all the various mental states: for
example, in the *waking* state, consciousness is the witness
of two simultaneous levels of activity: the internal one of
thoughts, imaginations, etc., and an external one of sense-
data from the "objective" world.

In the *dream* state, consciousness witnesses only on
the internal level, viewing the effusive activity of the
imagination known as dreams. And in the *deep-sleep*
state, consciousness finally gets a break, as there is nothing

at all to witness -- but Itself. When waking from this state, we say we were "unconscious," but actually, consciousness was not absent; what was absent was the thoughts, images, external sense-data, and dreams; i.e., the *seen*. Consciousness always remains; It is eternal. Even in deep-sleep, though It is devoid of witnessing-content, the *I* remains; otherwise, how would I recall when I awoke that *I* slept soundly?

There is yet another state of consciousness besides these three already mentioned: that is the state wherein consciousness transcends the Self-imposed limitation of a separate ego-identity -- the illusion of being confined to one particular body -- and recognizes Itself as universal. The *I* experienced in this state is not a different *I* from the one which has always been experienced; it is the same *I*, but happily divested of the wrong notion of who *I* is. We may call this state, *nirvana, samadhi, satori, the mystic marriage, oneness with God*, or whatever we like; it is, more precisely however, the startling experience of the expansion of one's consciousness from its limited personal identification to an unimaginably pure and lucid awareness that knows: *I am the one Consciousness of the universe! All this is my Self!*

Returning now to the idea prevalent in scientific circles that consciousness is somehow the product of the organization of matter: perhaps now we can understand that what we see in the evolutionary process is not a production of consciousness from the sufficiently complex organization of matter, but an *emergence* of Consciousness from a Self-imposed state of involution, a state of lesser Self-awareness, to an increasingly greater awareness of

Itself as the one Source and Substance of the entire universe. This is, indeed, the direction of all evolution.

The truth is that Consciousness is the *only* reality. It is both the *seer* and the *seen*; It manifests as the experiencing *I*, and It manifests as the wave-particles which we perceive as the world of "matter." It manifests as the *soul* of every sentient and insentient being, temporarily identifying with whatever form It takes; and, as the *soul* evolves in understanding over the period of numerous lifetimes, Consciousness studies Itself in the mirror of thought, mental tangles become unraveled, and eventually the nature of the Self becomes evident to Itself. Consciousness thus plays a game of hide-and-seek with Itself, manifesting initially in ignorance of Itself, and through the process of soul-evolution, finally awakening to Self-awareness. In Its universal Totality, It is always Self-aware; but in Its play as "matter" and "souls," It throws dust in Its own eyes for the sake of the game.

3. MIND

What, then, of the individual *mind*? If we define *mind* in the simplest possible way as the aggregate of thoughts experienced by an individual, it is not likely that anyone would deny that such a thing exists. Surely everyone can verify the existence of thoughts. Then the question arises, "What are thoughts?" And the answer given by the yogis and Vedantic philosophers is, "Thoughts are the vibrations (*vrittis*) of consciousness." We should take notice of the fact that thoughts, though registering as electrical energy on the EEG machines of psychological technicians, are formed of consciousness, and so must be understood as *both* consciousness and energy -- in the same way that a beam of light is understood to be both a stream of particles and also a propagation of waves.

One cannot categorize *mind* as only consciousness, or as only energy; it is both -- just as everything in this phenomenal universe is both. In fact, the manifestation of thoughts (i.e., *mind*) by our own individual consciousness is a process identical to the manifestation of the phenomenal universe by the universal Consciousness. In both cases, Consciousness projects a vibratory thought-force which appears as form; it is in this sense that man is said to be a reproduction of God, made in His image. The difference, of course, is that the private consciousness of man produces a privately perceived world of forms, whereas the universal Consciousness produces a universally perceived world of forms.

Man and his mind is God's miraculous projection of Himself and His Power into the world of His own Energy-creation. The attempt to analyze and define the *mind* any further is a fruitless endeavor, for the *mind* is, in the final analysis, only the *activity* of consciousness. It is much more pertinent to our advantage simply to recognize *who* we are, and to cease to identify with the creative effusion of our minds.

It is the common experience of everyone that thoughts continually arise on the surface of consciousness. Day and night, the activity of the mind is a reality that cannot be ignored. Nonetheless, the underlying consciousness remains as an unchanging background, an imperturbable witness, to the continuing play of thought. That pure sky of Consciousness will always remain -- long after the body has decayed, and the clouds of thought have dissolved. That pure Consciousness is the Self which you will always be -- unsullied, unaffected by even millions of births, and countless thoughts and dreams. Focusing one's attention on that Self has the effect of calming the stormy sea of thought, and allowing the peace, clarity and joy of pure *Awareness* to be experienced.

In the *Pratyabijnahridayam*, a philosophical tract of Kashmir Shaivism, it is said: "A man becomes bound through being deluded by his own *shakti*." In other words, by identifying with the contents of his own thought-activity (*mind*), and forgetting his permanent Identity, a man experiences himself as bound; and conversely, a man enjoys freedom simply by knowing that he is the one pure Consciousness, ever-free, ever-unaffected by the tumultuous activity of the *mind*. For this reason, the great medieval Indian sage, Shankaracharya, advised:

One should understand the Self to be distinct from the body, sense-organs, mind, intellect and instincts, and always a witness of their functions -- like a king [observing the activities of his kingdom].

One should know, "I am without attributes and actions, eternal, without doubts, unsullied, changeless, formless, ever-free and pure."

The constant awareness, "I am truly the Self" is the cure for the agitations caused by ignorance, just as medicine is the cure for disease. [5]

4. SOUL

It is necessary now to say something about the *soul*. The existence of thoughts, dreams, images, and psychic impressions reveals to us the existence of an aspect of Reality that is subtler than the physical phenomena experienced by the senses. God's *shakti*, or Power of creative Energy, if you prefer, has created a vaster spectrum of vibrations than just those perceived by the senses. An examination of the electromagnetic wave spectrum reveals a range of forty-four octaves, from ultra-violet light to long radio waves, of which only one octave is visible light. The *soul* also is of a subtler stuff than that we know as perceivable "matter."

However, not everyone agrees on just what the *soul* is. From the very remotest of ancient times it was evident to man that the principle of life was something separate from matter. For as long as that mysterious factor animated a body, it was alive and conscious; but when life departed, the body became a mere lump of decaying matter. Thus, it was apparent even to primitive man that the world consists of two separate principles: *spirit* and *matter*. Matter could be seen and touched, but the spirit of life was invisible and intangible; still, there was no denying that the *spirit* really existed, for it was obvious that a living body contained a definite something that was absent in a dead body; even a fool had to admit it. This invisible *spirit* of life was called by various names. To the Greek philosophers, it was *pneuma*, or *psyche*; to the Romans, it was *anima*, or *soul*.

To the philosophers and theologians of the West, this *soul* was conceived of as a concrete individual entity which retained its individualized existence for all eternity. But in the East, the *soul* (or *jīva*) is regarded as identical with the universal Self -- limited only by a false sense of individuality, or *ego*. This sense of individuality is regarded by Indian philosophers as a mere ignorance (*avidya*) of one's greater, universal Self. But this ignorance is not the ordinary kind of ignorance that can be easily remedied by the learning of facts; it is an ignorance that is "built-into" our human existence; in other words, it is an ignorance that is 'God-given,' and which can only be dispelled by His Grace, His Self-revelation. From this point of view, so long as the illusion of individuality exists, the *soul* exists; and only when this illusion is dispelled by the inner revelation of the universal Self, does the illusion of a separate *soul* cease to exist.

During the mystical experience of Unity, there is neither *soul* nor *God*, for that which imagines itself to be an individual *soul* becomes suddenly aware that it is the one and only Consciousness of the universe. In that pure Consciousness, there is no *soul*, no *God*; the polarization of subject-object exists only while the veil of ego-identification remains. This is not to say that the *soul* is unreal, a mere personal illusion, like a mirage; the soul is a manifestation of *Shakti*, or Divine Energy. If it is an illusion, it is an illusion produced by the supreme Consciousness; it is a product of His Divine Power of Illusion (*Maya*), and therefore is as real as any other of His manifestations. It continues its "illusory" existence for lifetime after lifetime, and ceases to exist only when He chooses to reveal Himself.

In every tradition of mystical philosophy -- whether Christian, Vedantic, Sufi, or pagan Greek -- we find complete agreement that the personality, the individual consciousness, of man is distinct from his physical body, and continues after the death of the physical body as a subtle form, or *soul*. There are differences among these traditions, however, as to how this *soul* comes to be and what happens to the *soul* after bodily death. According to those who believe the *soul* to be an eternally independent entity, there is a heavenly realm where *souls* dawdle away eternity enjoying pleasures of sense similar to those enjoyed during their sojurn on earth. According to the philosophy prevalent in the East, the *soul* may very well experience periods of "heavenly" or "purgatorial" respite, but then continues to take birth in new bodies, evolving in understanding and love till at last it experiences its Source, its universal Self; and then, after bodily death, continues to expand its universal awareness and love till it becomes entirely merged in and indistinguishable from the one Divine Consciousness. This is the view expressed in the *Upanishads*:

> As rivers flowing into the ocean find their final
> peace and their name and form disappear, even so the
> wise become free from name and form and enter into
> the radiance of the supreme Spirit. ... In truth, one who
> knows God becomes God. [6]

According to these ancient teachings, the *soul* does not reach its end in that perfect Purity, however, until it has rid itself of every impurity of ignorance, and is established in the awareness of the Self. And, as every soul must pass the same test of admittance to that realm of perfect Bliss, it is evident that, in the overall scheme, no possibility of injustice or favoritism exists. In a 'closed' evolutionary system such as this universe is, justice is complete and perfect; one cannot get out of it without going all the way to the end, and whatever wrong turnings are made along the way must be balanced exactly by corrections before the end can be reached.

To the ancient Greeks, this law of causality governing the subtle activity of the *soul* was known as *Adrasteia* (just retribution). It was supposed that, by virtue of this universal law, "we reap just what we sow." To the ancients of India, this principle was known as 'the law of *karma* ("actions").' Implicit in this law is the reincarnation of *souls* as often as needed to satisfy unfulfilled desires, right wrongs committed in the past, and evolve toward perfection.

But why does God become individualized *souls* in the first place? And were they all made at once or at various times? I don't know for sure; and I'm also not sure that "time" is a relevant concept in regard to the subtle level of Consciousness in which all events are contained in the eternal "present." And, judging by the variety of explanations available on the origin and destiny of souls, it would seem that no one really knows for sure how or why this process of individuation comes about.

We can only surmise that it is the sport, or play, of the one Consciousness. But I do know one thing for sure: that the dawning of enlightenment, the vision of ultimate Unity, puts an end to the conceit of individuation, and what we call the *soul*; for the final truth is that there is only one *I* who is playing all the parts of all the *souls*. And the realization of this is what is referred to in the scriptures as "liberation" from the wheel of rebirth:

The realization of one's identity with Brahman is the
cause of liberation from the bondage of rebirth, by
means of which the wise man attains Brahman, the One
without a second, absolute Bliss. It is this supreme
Oneness which alone is real, since there is nothing else
but the Self. Truly, there remains no other independent
entity in the state of the realization of supreme Truth. [7]

5.   THE PROBLEM OF EVIL

This brings us to consider the question of why, if the one Self is acting in and as all souls, does He so often make disastrous choices and commit heinously wrong acts? Why, in short, is there *evil* in the world?

To answer this question, we must understand the evolutionary nature of *Shakti*. *Shakti*, God's power of manifestation, produces a drama which unfolds from a simple unity to a vast multiplicity -- from the first stirring of Desire, to the formation of particles, to the structuring of chemical elements, to simple life-forms, to mammals, to primates, to man, and ultimately to Self-realization. This is the process of soul-evolution. Inherent in all of *Shakti's* effulgent production is the one Consciousness of which *Shakti* is the manifestation; It exists in and as every particle and force in the universe -- as the interstellar dust, as the rocks, as the plants, as the microbes, and so on. However, Self-awareness is merely latent, potential, until it has a fully developed human soul through which to function.

The ape is conscious; the dog is conscious; but not until the soul evolves to its fullest capability as man does Consciousness manifest Its full potential and become aware of Itself. All life is therefore an evolutionary game of knowledge-gathering toward the end of becoming fully developed and able to directly perceive the answer to the puzzling question, "Who am I?" And this does not occur until man reaches his highest stage -- requiring a moral and intellectual development that can only be acquired over the period of many human lifetimes.

This leads us to the answer to our original question about evil: In the process of evolution, while men are as yet unaware of their universal Identity, mistakes occur, wrong choices are made -- just as children growing up make many mistakes before they reach adulthood. During this necessary process of evolution, mistakes based on an ignorance of the nature of reality can be extremely cruel and horrible -- evil, in fact.

The will to act on such wrong understanding results in evil acts. These are not acts of a truly "free" will, for it is only the pure mind, freed of ignorance, that is able to act from a clear, considered awareness of what is correct action and what is not, what stems from the illusory ego for personal satisfaction, and what stems from a divine will for the greater good of all. "Free-will" is nothing but the will of God *freed* of the passions and impulses arising from the false ego. The so-called "free-will" of the murderer or thief is not a "free" will at all, but one that is constricted and obscured by the false sense of ego and its attendant desires.

There is no question that cruel and evil acts do occur during the process of *Shakti's* unfolding, but it is just as certain that, in the completion of the evolutionary process, all evils and injustices become justly resolved. On the subtle level of the soul, these resolutions occur by a reformation of the heart, or we might say, of the soul itself. There is no end to the soul's journeying until, after many lifetimes, it has become "perfect as the Father is perfect."

The same law of causality which is operative on the physical level is active on the soul level as well; we are able to reach the happiness of our true Self only by the perfection of our souls. It is in this sense that we reap just what we sow. For, just as the refinement of gold requires the burning of all impurities, likewise, the soul does not reach its final stage of Purity until it has passed through the fire of remorse and correction which burns away all evil propensities, and until it has been proved worthy in the discerning eye of our own divine Self who witnesses all.

'All's well that ends well,' it's truly said; for the consummation of the evolutionary process -- the knowledge and awareness of our true, universal Self -- reveals that the process of evolution is only a flimsy masquerade, that in fact we have *always* been free, always been Divine and completely unaffected by the drama of *Shakti's* unfolding. It is true that evil exists in the process of evolution; but He who is projecting that drama is ever beyond good and evil, pain and pleasure; and that is who -- it must one day be realized -- we are.

If we see truly, we must see that we cannot fail to reach eventually to our highest potential; for He, as us, will continue to choose according to the degree of our understanding. He will keep on striving, as us, to more thoroughly eliminate all error from our endeavors. It is His drama, and each act will unfold according to His script and His direction. It is He who is acting out all the parts, as us, and experiencing all the joys and sorrows as well as the transcendence of them. There is no advice to offer, no corrections to make; He is already in charge. He will continue to enliven our minds, to inspire our intellects, to illumine our souls. It is to ourselves that we must and will be true, for it is as our *Self* that He will lead us unerringly on our uniquely special way.

6. PERSONALITY

The soul in the above context is really identical with personality. What I mean by the word, *personality*, is the sum total of those qualities that go to make up the uniqueness of an individual, the stamp of individuality which marks each being as a specific and unique person. But why this abundance of individual personalities? How account for the amazing variety of personal charactistics possessed by each soul?

I would like to offer an hypothesis, along with a warning: what follows is heady stuff, quite beyond what nearly everyone believes, and may be shockingly unbelievable to the minds of those who are convinced that they already fully understand everything in the universe. Conventional minds may elect to disregard and pass over this chapter; but for those who are open to giving fair hearing to even the most outrageous hypotheses, I offer the following:

Let us suppose that each personality/soul corresponds to the planetary architecture existing in the heavens at the time of its terrestrial birth, and is merely an expression of the universal energy-pattern existing at that moment in the evolution of space-time. Just as the destined role of an atom is determined by the overall structure or chemical organization of the whole organism of which it is a part, is it not also possible that each individual soul, or personality, fits precisely into a larger overall scheme which demands its appearance at precisely the time and place, and under the precise circumstances, established for it; so that it is sent forth into the world on cue in perfect correspondence with the planetary arrangement which defines its being?

Throughout known history discerning men who have studied the heavens have asserted that something like this was indeed the case, that a person's characteristics and destiny were written in the stars, and that a wise person who was able to read the symbols of that language could thereby read the secrets of human souls. On this very supposition, three Persian astrologers set out, long ago, for Bethlehem, aware that whoever was going to be born at that place at that time was undoubtedly a great being with a great destiny; for it was foretold in the extraordinary configurations of the planets about to appear.

The discovery of astrology -- the understanding of the relationship of planetary positions to the nature of each individual human soul and its destiny -- seems to have first occurred among the Chaldeans, a highly advanced people who, according to legend, had mapped out the constellations as we know them today by the year 2800 B.C.E., and had already gathered centuries of scientific observations of the movements of the planets, enabling them to draw charts or "horoscopes" ("to see the hour") for the birth of its citizens.

Babylon, following their influence, was said by Cicero to have spent 470 years in collecting observations of the history of children born under particular combinations of heavenly bodies in order to perfect their astrological knowledge. This knowledge in turn was adopted and refined by the Persians, whose adepts were known as *Magi*. And throughout the West this knowledge was disseminated by the Arabs and Indian sages, resulting in its popularization in medieval Europe. But with the decline of

philosophical learning and the rise of materialism and its
technology in the West, astrology became, for a time, a lost
art.

Today, however, there is a new renaissance of
mysticism in the West fostered by the influence of Eastern
thought, and it is in this climate of renewed interest in the
subtleties of natural philosophy that the ancient principles
of cosmic correspondence have re-emerged into the light.
For the past half-century, many great minds have
contributed to the elaboration and validation of the secrets
of that most ancient of all sciences. And today, there is a
growing segment of professionals, including many
practicing Psychologists, who routinely counsel their clients
on the basis of a thorough study of their "natal horoscope,"
the chart of the planetary positions at the time and place of
that individual's birth.

Such a chart is, in effect, a still-frame picture of one
moment in the history of the universe. It marks an exact
and unique event in the unfolding of the universe of time
and space which occurs only once. For that reason, it is an
absolutely accurate indicator of the nature of life at that
particular moment and place (whether we may be capable
of accurately reading it or not). The creature born at that
juncture is, in a sense, an embodiment of the very unique
arrangement of the stellar and planetary bodies existing at
that particular "frame" in the unfoldment of the universe.
The positions of the heavenly bodies are therefore related
to the person born at a particular moment, not in any
causal way, but simply by virtue of the fact that they are
each embodiments of the same moment in the coordinated
unfolding of the universe.

7. THE CELESTIAL
DYNAMICS OF GRACE

Nearly ten years had passed since my experience of enlightenment in the Santa Cruz mountains, when I began to be interested in the peculiar claims of astrology, and came to have an understanding of the "celestial dynamics," not only of my own personal characteristics, but of all the ordinary and extraordinary day-to-day transient conditions of the mind, the body, and the soul. There were, no doubt, some "celestial influences" accompanying that dawning interest in astrological correspondences, but all I knew was that I had become facinated with the clearly meaningful connections between my own natal planetary positions and my personal characteristics and fluctuating mental states; and as I eagerly consumed what literature I found on the subject, I became more and more convinced of the validity of the astrological principle of correspondence between the planetary positions and the varying conditions of my psyche.

According to the principles of astrology, one can discover the secrets of a soul's unique characteristics (the psychology of a personality) by drawing a map of the heavens as it appeared at the exact moment and place of birth, which serves as a sort of blueprint of that particular soul. But how, when, and in what sequence the events of the person's adventure on earth will take place is told in the *progressions* of the planets (one day in the ephemeris represents one year in the life), and by the daily *transits* (actual transitory positions) of the Sun, moon and planets as they pass through and relate to the natal map.

All of the planets move (transit) through the twelve signs of the zodiac which comprise the 360º of the ecliptic; some slowly, some more rapidly. The Sun moves approximately one degree per day, and the moon one degree approximately every two hours. The outer planets take weeks or months to move through a degree. But always the overall architecture of this "atom" which we call the solar system is altering its design moment by moment. And we, who are within the confines of this "atom" are continually experiencing the changes in our own energy-patterns according to, and corresponding with, the changes in the angles from which the various planets and stars relate to us.

This implies, of course, that *everything* that happens to us in our lives will be accompanied by a planetary arrangement which, in its relationship to the positions of the planets at the moment of our birth, will symbolize that event. One day, it occurred to me that, if these principles were true, there would have to have been a configuration in the progressed and transitting positions of the planets on the night of my "mystical experience" that was significantly extraordinary. In other words, that Divine experience which we refer to as "*grace*" must also have been signified in the planetary patterns in effect for me on that very night.

This was a mind-boggling concept that was to stand many of my most cherished presumptions on their heads. In order to explain why this should be so, let me take a moment to describe some of those presumptions regarding that mysterious thing called "grace," which is, from the standpoint of its recipient, a new and radical change in consciousness, and, subsequently, in the personality, which arises seemingly from out of nowhere:

From the moment my soul first awakened with "spiritual" understanding, and the love and desire for God first entered my heart, I had attributed that awakening to God's grace. And there was no question in my mind that my later, "mystical," experience was the gift of grace, for there was absolutely no denying the fact that this experience had been *given* to me. I had not earned it; I had practiced no technique, no method; by no means could I be said to have produced it. There was no other word to describe this gift other than "grace."

Traditionally, grace -- the grace of God -- was thought of as the freely given intercession of God to a humbled soul, lifting it momentarily to mergence in the universal Consciousness. In this experience, the false, but insistent, illusion of a separate soul-identity, or ego, is dissolved, and the Divine Intelligence which is the infinite and eternal Self of all is revealed. How could the illusory, individual, self imagine that it had accomplished this feat? Let those who think they can accomplish it do so. When the Self is realized, that separate self is no longer even there! The eternal Self appears only at its demise. And it has not the ability to slay itself; it is only the divine revelation of God that, in an instant, dissolves that tenacious illusory ego. It is grace.

Listen to what that enlightened 15th-century monk, Thomas á Kempis, had to say about grace:

> When spiritual comfort is sent to you of God, take it meekly and give thanks humbly for it. But know for certain that it is of the great goodness of God that it is

sent to you, and not of your deserving. And see that you
are not lifted up therefore unto pride, nor that you joy
much thereof, nor presume vainly therein, but rather
that you be the more meek for so noble a gift, and the
more watchful and fearful in all your works; for that
time will pass away, and the time of temptation will
shortly follow after. When comfort is withdrawn,
despair not therefore, but meekly and patiently await the
visitation of God, for He is able and of sufficient power
to give you more grace and more spiritual comfort than
you had first.

Such alteration of grace is no new thing, and no
strange thing to those who have had experience in the
way of God; for in all great saints and in all lovers of
God similar alteration has often been found.

... If almighty God has done thus with holy saints, it
is not for us, weak and feeble persons, to despair, though
we sometimes have fervor of spirit, and are sometimes
left cold and void of devotion. *The Spirit comes and
goes according to His pleasure,* and therefore Job
said: "Lord, Thou graciously visitest Thy lover in the
morning, that is to say, in the time of comfort; and
suddenly Thou provest him in withdrawing such
comforts from him."

... He who knows the comforts that come through
the gift of grace and knows also how sharp and painful
the absenting of grace is, shall not dare think that any
goodness comes of himself; but he shall openly confess
that of himself he is very poor and naked of all virtue. [8]

What Thomas said conformed to my own experience.
The fervor of devotion was not always the same; it came
and went, apparently according to its own pleasure.
Likewise, the clarity of understanding was sometimes
absent, and at other times inspiration seemed to flood my
mind with the wisdom of God. One day I might be filled

with love and fervor; another day I might be dry or
lethargic, or physically energetic, or contemplative. One
day I might be bubbling with creative energy; another day I
would be dry as a bone. There was no telling what kind of
inner state each day would bring.

The experience of union, or Unity, had come to me only
once. Why on that day, at that time? I could only explain
it, as Thomas á Kempis did, as God's inexplicable grace.
But now I was beginning to understand something of the
celestial dynamics of grace, i.e., the principles of astrological correspondence. And so I drew up a chart for that
night of November 18, 1966.

What a revelation it was when I beheld that chart! The
correspondence was undeniable. Here before my eyes was
clear and unequivocal proof of the "science" of astral
correspondences. Any impartial astrologer viewing the
progressions and transits to my natal chart which occurred
on that evening would have to acknowledge that this was
indeed a night of destiny, an undeniably magical night of
mystical vision, a once-in-a-lifetime night of incredible
potential for the meeting with God. The extraordinary
emphasis on the planetary position of Neptune (known as
the planet of mystical experience) at that particular time is
eloquently conclusive.

If -- as many people think -- there is really no
correlation between the planets and the human psyche,
then what an extraordinarily grand coincidence it was,
what a marvellous accident of nature, that at the same
moment that I was experiencing the Godhead, the planets
were proclaiming it in the heavens! I think any reasonable
person with even a little astrological acumen, on viewing
the "influences" in effect for me that night, would have to

acknowledge that the significant planetary picture at the time of my "enlightenment experience" does, in fact, seem to provide evidence of the validity of the contents of that experience, confirming that all things do indeed "move together of one accord," that nothing happens that is not ordained to happen, that the universe is one coordinated Whole. *(For details on the Astrological conditions existing at the time of my "Enlightenment," see the Appendix at the back of the book.)*

But, along with the excitement of discovery and validation which I felt on viewing this chart, there was a nagging question that left me baffled and confused: If this "mystical experience" was described in the heavens since the beginning of time, and therefore entirely predestined, where was "grace"? Where was the freely-given gift of God that I had experienced as occurring at just that moment? If everything was strictly predetermined, where was grace and free-will and the possibility of spiritual endeavor?

Where was choice or merit or virtue? Where was blame or culpability? And where was the hope or possibility of "spiritual experience" for those in whose astrological forecast the prerequisite planetary conditions were *not* present? If God's universe is merely the mechanistic unfolding of an undeviating script, then are we all merely mechanical pawns, and our trials and triumphs, our perseverings and defeats, merely dramatic plot-twists in a story that's already written, typeset and published?

It is important to emphasize at this time that the planets, in themselves, do not have the power to *cause* either good or ill-fortune, though many (including myself) habitually speak of "planetary influences" as though they were *independent causes* determining our fate. In ancient times, of course, as planetary configurations were seen to correspond to definite kinds of psychological and behavioral effects, the naive supposed that planets were therefore independent forces, responsible for the destiny of man. Each planet was fitted out with its own individual personality, and was assumed to have independent power to affect events on earth. This was the basis for the myths of the "gods."

The great Roman mystic, Plotinus, writing in the 3rd century C.E. on the subject of *Are The Stars Causes?*, noted that a belief in the independent power of the planets is "tenable only by minds ignorant of the [true] nature of a Universe which has a ruling Principle and a First Cause operative downward through every member."[9] He explained:

> Each [planetary] entity takes its origin from one Principle and, therefore, while executing its own function, works in with every other member of that All.
> ... And there is nothing undesigned, nothing of chance, in all the process: all is one scheme of differentiation, starting from the First Cause and working itself out in a continuous progression of effects. [10]

This perfectly unfolding progression of effects from the one all-ruling Cause is clearly seen by all who have been graced with "the vision of God." It is that "vision" which is the experiential basis for the assertion that "all things move together of one accord"; that "assent is given throughout the universe to every falling grain." Still, the question of *how* the transitting "planetary influences" operate, i.e., by what process Neptune or any other planet transmits to individual souls its effects, is a legitimate one. And the matter of how *progressions* operate (which are not even present-time events, but "symbols" of planetary events already past) is even more perplexing. These questions cannot be answered by present-day knowledge, but many astrologers guess that something like the following is the case:

As the planets of the solar system change their angles to one another and thus rearrange the structural design of the entire system and its relationship to the design at one's nativity, there is a corresponding change in the pattern of conscious energy (*Shakti*) which makes up our psychic and phenomenal reality. The energy-pattern (produced by the angular positions of the Sun, Moon and planets) which exists at the time of an individual's birth, corresponds to the conscious energy-pattern, or aggregation of qualities, of that individual soul. And the subsequent alterations of the planetary positions after that moment spell out in decipherable terms his or her destiny.

It seems to me, however, that the search for a *cause-effect* relationship between the transits and progressions of planets and the lives of individual souls on earth is indicative of humanity's long-standing mistaken view of reality. Plotinus saw in the 2nd century what is true eternally -- that there is *one* Cause, and all else is Its effects. The planets do not focus beneficent or malevolent rays or forces in our direction; they do not put forth any fields of influence that impinge on us at all. In short, they are not causes at all, but merely *signs* of the activity of the one Cause which is God, revealed to those who can read them.

I believe it is very important to understand that, although the planets *signal* psychic and physical events experienced on earth, they are not themselves responsible;

they are not the *cause*, but are only coincident effects synchronous with the effects perceived upon earthly life. In short, the "influences" of the planets are really the influences of the unbroken Whole, manifesting locally as specific patterns of relationships. The planets do not determine our fate; they merely reveal it. Our lives are determined by the One in whom the planets move. This is a view consistent with the view of Plotinus, and I believe it will be consistent with the enlightened understanding of the future.

The evolution of the soul occurs over many lifetimes, with its summit being the full openness to self-surrender in the Love of God, and the subsequent realization of its supreme Identity. And because the evolution of the universe reflects the evolution of each soul, the stellar and planetary positions which signal that soul's enlightenment will coincide perfectly with that moment in the soul's evolutionary summit. And the question of whether it is the soul's evolutionary struggle or the planetary alignments which brings about enlightenment must be answered, "Neither." They are coordinated events in the unfolding of God's cosmic drama; both events are simultaneous effects of the one Cause, occurring in Himself in the ordered unfoldment of His will. All is one coordinated whole, and all that occurs within it is a manifestation of His grace.

The complexity of such a universe -- a universe in which the destiny of each succeeding manifestation of a soul on earth is in synchronization with the ongoing motions of planetary bodies -- is indeed beyond our present ability to conceive or visualize. Nonetheless, we must acknowledge that it is impossible to separate the birth of any individual from the cosmic conditions in which it occurs. For the universe is an integral Whole, and every event in it is in interlocking agreement with every other; not even the tiniest, most seemingly insignificant, event may be considered as an isolated phenomenon.

Within this Whole, where "all things move together of one accord," the division of small-scale events into categories of *cause* and *effect* is imaginary and has no real meaning. For it is the Lord, God, *Shiva* -- call Him what you will -- who, by means of His Power of Will (*Shakti*), is the sole Cause of the entire manifested array of the cosmos and therefore of every single event which takes place within it. This truth is seen clearly and unmistakably in the unitive experience of the mystic.

8. FREEDOM OR DETERMINISM?

This startling empirical evidence of an astrological correspondence to the experience of enlightenment leads us to some unavoidable conclusions: It appears evident that enlightenment, the vision of God -- whatever we may wish to call it -- is a fated and determined event. This is a staggering thought! "Well," you may ask, "Can grace be a predetermined event? Is enlightenment merely a matter of fate?" These questions are not easy to answer, but I will try: From our limited viewpoint in time, the experience of unity appears to be a product of instantaneous grace. But *time*, from the viewpoint of eternal Being, is another thing altogether. To It, the entire universal cycle, from "Big Bang" to final implosion, is but the blinking of an eye, the rising and falling of a breath; and the universe, including all our experiences within it, evolves according to the undeviating law of causal progression. All things do indeed move together of one accord; and there is no event, however subtle, that is not determined from the first by God, who is the ultimate Cause.

Frequently it happens that those who commit themselves to a life of devotion and service to God do so at a time when they are newly awakened by grace. That amazing grace is experienced as a suddenly growing intensity of their experience of the Divine presence in their lives and a fervent clarity of their inner vision. No doubt some heavenly body (or bodies) is beginning at that time to enter into a significant relationship with Neptune's place in the pattern of planetary positions existent at their birth. Perhaps, at the moment that body (or bodies) culminates its relationship to Neptune's natal position, they will have a profound experience of the One as their own eternal Self.

Then, as time passes, those who once thrilled to the touch of God's invisible hand and peered into the infinite peace and wonder of God's eternal Self no longer feel the nearness of His presence nor any longer see with the same clarity. It may be that they will come to feel that God has abandoned them, or that perhaps they have gone astray and are being punished for their infidelity. No doubt, they will long for those earlier days when their thoughts never strayed from His praise and their hearts were never without the fullness of Divine love, when they were consumed with selfless desire for His enveloping embrace.

But the heavens change, and the earth spins on through endless space, and the celestial influence which God once brought to pass in their lives moves on to affect and inspire another. God has not withdrawn His grace; it was but a momentary opening of the aperture of the psyche, a glimpse into the eternal Source, signified by the momentary arrangement of the ever-changing positions of the planets, stars and galaxies in this fathomless universe as they relate to this one human entity in time and space.

In short, that receptivity, that mysterious opening of awareness, that drawing of the human heart and mind to immersion and complete abnegation in the heart and mind of that universal Being which we call God was coincident with the conditions occurring in the natural unfolding of God's universal drama, of which He is the producer, director, stage, actors, and scenery. In short, it was His gift, His grace. It was He who planted that moment in amongst all the moments, that arrangement in amongst all the possible arrangements of the heavenly bodies in the universe, and that "mystical" experience in amongst all the experiences known to man. What else shall we call it but His grace? And what are all other moments, arrangements and experiences that follow in a lifetime but His grace as well?

As for the question of man's 'free-will' in a universe entirely determined by the will of God, the nineteenth century saint, Sri Ramakrishna, perhaps the greatest mystic and seer the world has ever known, had this to say:

> The Englishman [i.e., the Western materialist] talks about free-will, but those who have realized God are aware that free-will is a mere appearance. In reality, man is the machine and God is the Operator. Man is the carriage and God its Driver. [11]

Still, you may object to what is seen as a world of strict determination, and ask, "If every event in our lives is determined by God, where, then is our freedom of choice? Where is the possibility for virtue, for choosing the path of righteousness over the path of evil? And how is it even possible to progress spiritually by one's own efforts if all is in God's hands? How can we be held responsible for our acts if every sentiment, emotion, thought, or act is determined by God?"

These are questions which must occur to anyone who thinks deeply about such matters. But these questions are framed on a presumption of duality where none in fact exists. For *we* and *God* are ultimately not two. And it is only a linguistic quandary that we fall into when we regard ourselves and God as separate entities, and consider one to be determining the other. There is only One in this universe; it is *He* who, *as us*, is freely making all the choices.

Each individual being (soul) chooses according to his or her evolutionary development, but it is He alone who is manifesting as each individual at every step on the evolutionary scale. Therefore, we must admit that everything is determined by God's Will. And ... we must also see that, since we are Him, we are free to choose. When these two, man and God, are recognized to be one, this question of whether we are free or determined in our willing is easily resolved: Determinism and free-will are *both* true; they are "complementary" truths, each representing one aspect of a dual-sided reality. As the one eternal Consciousness, beyond time, we are forever free; as individualzed souls, in time, we are determined by the law of causality, and are therefore under the decree of fate.

Thus, the question, "Are we responsible for our acts?" must be answered, "No," from the standpoint of our individualized souls; and "Yes," from the standpoint of the Self. For, as the one Consciousness, we are the witness of all the thoughts and impulses of our nature, and are free to grant or withhold consent to her promptings. Therefore, ultimately, we *are* responsible for our acts. It is on the basis of our Divinity that all civil and criminal law intuitively recognizes the culpability of the individual. For, if we were not the eternal Self in essence, if we were not absolutely free from causal necessity, but merely unwitting, mechanical pawns, we could not be held responsible for what we do. But our Self *is* God, we *are* free; and therefore, we *are* responsible.

The question of "free-will" is one which has facinated the minds of men since first man looked to the heavens and deduced a Creator. And, though the answer to the problem is very simple, it is difficult for most minds to assimilate which have not gotten into the habit of allowing for two answers to be true which contradict each other. Such an attitude is required of physicists for whom light, and energy itself, must be seen as both a particle (quanta) and a wave, whose respective qualities are mutually exclusive. What is required is the ability to freely shift one's viewpoint from one frame of reference to another.

The answer to the question, "Do I have free-will?" is determined by who *I* is; in other words, to which "I" you are referring. If you are identifying with the body, mind and soul, the answer is, "No, you do not have free-will." Nothing happens in this drama that was not in the original script. Omar Khayyam has rightly said: "The first morning of creation wrote what the last dawn of reckoning shall read." The Will that flung forth the universe is its only Cause, and all that follows is effect. All effects are implied and contained in their cause, as the tree is contained in its seed. Even your apparent choosing is *His* choosing; even the choosing is Him. In short, there is no escaping Him, for He is "even that which thinks of escape."

On the other hand, if by *I* you refer to the one Self, the universal Consciousness; if by *I* you mean the eternal Lord and Witness of all this drama, then you already know the answer: "Yes, you have free-will. Your will is the only will; You are Freedom itself!"

∞   ∞   ∞

PART FOUR:

The Worship Of The Self

"Of all the means to liberation, devotion is the highest.

"To seek earnestly to know one's real nature -- this is said to be devotion." [1]

-- Shankaracharya,
Vivekachudamani

"Devotion consists of supreme love for God. It is nectar. On obtaining it, man has achieved everything; he becomes immortal; he is completely satisfied.

"Having attained it, he desires nothing else, he strives for nothing else. Having realized that supreme Love, a man becomes as if intoxicated; he delights only in his own intrinsic bliss." [2]

-- Narada,
Bhakti Sutras

1. THE APPEARANCE OF DUALITY

The two quotations which preface this section -- one by Shankaracharya, and the other by the legendary saint, Narada -- recommend precisely the same devotion to the very same Reality; but see how different are the words each of these men use: one speaks of earnestly seeking "to know one's real nature," while the other extols "love for God." Shankaracharya defines devotion as "continual meditation on one's own true Self"; and Narada, recognized as the greatest ancient authority on the philosophy of love, declares devotion to be "the constant flow of love towards the Lord." These two paths, of course, are not in any way different from one another; meditation on the Self *is* the love of God. It is only that Shankaracharya identifies with the Self, while Narada prefers to identify with the soul (*jiva*). Both are methods of focusing upon the one Reality, and each, inevitably, produces the same result.

Nonetheless, this complementarity of identities necessitates two entirely different mental attitudes, or states of awareness. When we focus on the Self, we are focusing on our own identity, and become aware: *I am the one infinite Existence-Consciousness-Bliss.* But when we take the attitude of love toward God, we are focusing on That which is other than ourself, and become aware: *I am Thy creature and Thy servant, O Lord.* And it is the paradoxical fact that both attitudes are correct and valid which accounts for the confused oscillation many dedicated truth-seekers feel between the attitude of Self-knowledge (*jnan*) and the attitude of devotion (*bhakti*).

Devotion may be thought of as the love of the soul for God; i.e., a relationship requiring two parties. For that reason, devotion is considered a 'Dualistic' practice. The entire Judeo-Christian tradition, as well as the Muslim and Hindu traditions in their popular form, are fundamentally dualistic in nature; that is, they take as their starting point the distinction between God and the created universe. This naturally implies a distinction as well between God and the created soul. These two they regard as intrinsically separate, and the objective of their practice is to unite the one to the other.

However, there are some other religious traditions which seem to practioners of devotion to be entirely alien to religion altogether, as they only profess to seek knowledge of the Self. Such other traditions, like the yogic, the Vedantic, and the Buddhist, in their esoteric form, are 'Non-Dualistic'; that is, they take as their starting point the non-difference between the individual's identity and the Cosmic Identity. Their practice is intended to uncover or reveal the underlying unity of the individual self and the universal Self. Put a little differently, they seek to reveal the Divine Identity inherent within us all.

Both of these religious practices -- the dualistic which aspires to union with the Divine Reality through prayer, and the non-dualistic which aspires to revelation of identity with the Divine Reality through meditation -- are capable of bringing the practioner to the realization of the Divine Reality, the ultimate Truth. Yet, how alien to each other are these two practices, or paths! How can we ever hope to reconcile these two, so fundamentally opposed to one another? The dualistic path of devotion (*bhakti*) is the path taken by the soul in search of God. Whereas, the non-dualistic path of knowledge (*jnan*) does not even acknowledge the reality of the soul, but clings steadfastly to the identification with the one Divine Self, the true Reality. How different these two paths seem! How could anyone possibly assert that they have anything in common?

And yet, look more closely at the actual process that takes place within the devotee and the jnani. When we call to God, where is it we look for His answer? Is it not within ourself? It is not in some external location high above that we seek God's presence, but rather we turn our eyes upward within ourselves to our own highest consciousness. At the initial, mental, level, the soul busily pleads and prays to God; but at a more profound level it simply calls His Name within, or merely searches the inner sky in silence, awaiting the balm of His peace, His love, to have its affect within.

The love of God looks to the center of one's own consciousness, raises to the greatest height one's inner gaze in search of That which is beyond the activity of the mind, beyond the critical intellect, beyond the searching soul, at the hidden core of being and awareness. This, too, is where the eye of knowledge looks for Him: beyond the concerns for self that form as thoughts and dreams, in the silence of an inward wakeful gaze unobstructed by the clouded haze of memories or fantasies. It scans the heart of darkness, and becomes enraptured in the upward-streaming light.

At the mental, conceptual, level, the love of God, with all its moods and bargainings, is quite a different thing from the meditation on the Self, which is quiet, empty, unwavering, keenly discriminative. It is only when each reaches to a level of nonverbal sweetness, high above the bustling commerce of the mind, above the conniving of the intellect, and the self-involvement of the soul, that the two paths become single, oned in a common stream of upward-flowing joy which knows no separation, knows no duality of kind or purpose.

And so, while each of these methods of reaching to the ultimate Truth are separate and distinct, and manifest in extremely diverse ways at the mental level, their differences dissolve and their divergent methods converge as they near the object of their quest. In the high reaches of the mountain's peak, all paths must come to a single point; likewise, when the lover and the meditator come to taste the silent Bliss that characterizes the approachment to the pinnacle of Truth, they have entered the subtle and ethereal realm where love and knowledge are one. Here, there is no distinction such as lover and knower; here is only the eternally blissful and all-inclusive 'I', who is neither God nor self.

During the time I spent in my Santa Cruz cabin, I had a photo of the *jnani*, Ramana Maharshi, on one wall, and a picture of the *bhakta,* Sri Ramakrishna, on the other wall. At one time, I would feel entirely committed to the continued awareness of my identity with infinite unqualified Consciousness, and would identify with Ramana, whose *sadhana* consisted of questioning within "Who am I?" At another time, I would feel certain that devotional love for God was the only attitude for me, and I would identify with Sri Ramakrishna, who was the simple child of God, crying for his Divine 'Mother'. And although the duality between the 'soul' and 'God' is, ultimately, an imaginary, or artificial, duality, still it exists so long as the active mind dialogues with that 'other'.

I knew, intellectually, that the duality between "me" and "God" was an artificial one. I knew that to take the attitude of love for God required a sort of pretense of "two-ness"; but the very existence of the active mind demanded such a relationship. In order to disengage my mind from its aimless wandering and to focus it on the eternal Silence, I had to have a point of focus, and that point of focus was that infinite Intelligence which I addressed as "Hari." Yes, I knew that this ego-self was included in and inseparable from that greater Self, but I also knew instinctually that, if I was to truly *know* the eternal Truth, I had to turn away from conceptual knowledge and concentrate with all the yearning of my soul on that pure and silent Awareness that lived beyond the active mind.

For me, it was love that ushered in the knowledge of the eternal Self; it was love which erased the sense of individual selfhood, allowing the true Self to be revealed. Previous to that unitive revelation, I sought God as a servant, as a soul at the feet of my Lord and Creator, feeling the delicious yet still distant presence of His love and guidance within me. "I" was this separate person, living in the wilderness, and "He" was the Divine Source of all, to whom I prayed, and who I sought to know through submission to His Will and through the continual remembrance of His presence in and as the world about me.

In the nights, prior to my experience of "enlight-enment," when I was finished with my daily tasks, I'd earnestly await Him in the silence by the glowing fire, making my awareness keenly receptive of His coming. In the evening twilight, I'd sing to Him, to the tune of *Danny Boy*:

> O Adonai, at last the day is dying;
> My heart is stilled as darkness floods the land.
> I've tried and tried, but now I'm through with
>   tryin';
> It's You, it's You, must take me by the hand,
> And lead me home where all my tears and
>   laughter
> Fade into bliss on Freedom's boundless shore.
> And I'll be dead and gone forever after;
> O Adonai, just You, just You alone,
> forevermore.

Or, sometimes, I'd sing this song, to the tune of *Across The Wide Missouri*:

> O Adonai, I long to see you!
> All the day, my heart is achin'.
> O Adonai, my heart is achin';
> O where, O where are you?
> Don't leave me here forsaken.
>
> O Adonai, the day is over;
> Adonai, I'm tired and lonely.
> My tears have dried, and I'm awaitin'
>   You; O Adonai,
> You know I love you only.

To focus my mind on Him, to bring devotion to my sometimes dry and empty heart, I'd read from Thomas á

Kempis' *Imitation Of Christ* -- a version which I had pared down from the original; and this had the invariable effect of lifting my heart to love of God, and brought me, as though by sympathetic resonance, to the same sweet simple devotion and purity of heart evidenced by that sweet monk of the 15th century. I felt so much kinship with him, so much identification with him, that I came to love his little book above all other works for its sweet effect on me.

But, after I was blessed with enlightenment on that November night, I tore that once favored book a handful of pages at a time from its binding, and fed those pages to the fire in my stove. Why? Because it was now clear that the duality of "me" and "Him" was a charade, a flimsy myth of 'two-ness' that had been discredited and burst asunder by the revelation of the unitive Self. That illusion of duality had been necessary to bring me to the point of perfect love, to open my mind and heart to the "vision"; but once revealed, that Unity swept away all previous delusion of a separate individual identity.

I think that, for many of us mortals, the devotional path is the only way we can reach enlightenment. And yet, ultimately, it is a path that is false in nearly all of its assumptions. The experience of Unity reveals that there were never two, that the prolonged and agonizing dialogue and relationship with God was an "imaginary" relationship. The One we call "I" was always the only one who ever was.

However, long after the destruction of my beloved *Imitation Of Christ*, I came to see that, even after the realization of the eternal Self, there persists the stubborn habits of thought and the convincing sense of bodily separateness and individuality. I came to see that the Self, the One, insists on taking the role of both God and devotee in order to enjoy the relationship of loving soul to loving God. Whether we like it or not, the One will not be denied the enjoyment of playing this game of duality with Himself; and so there is no way to avoid this dualistic drama of devotion.

I had been shown that the consciousness that lived in this body, that animated the thoughts that arose as wisdom, and moved this body and all bodies -- that consciousness was, and had always been, the one Consciousness that filled all things. I was not merely the wave; I was the Ocean. But the wave continued to exist! I was not simply the Ocean; I was the wave as well. I was a *jnani,* but I was still a *bhakta* as well.

I came to understand that there are two identities living within every individual: there is an eternal and unchanging Consciousness, the Witness, the true Self; and there is a superimposed ego-identity called 'the soul', which is a contracted and separate self with individual desires and goals. This superimposed self is of the stuff of dreams; it is real enough to go on evolving through numerous lifetimes, but it is ultimately imaginary, and must eventually be dispelled. It is dispelled only when the truth of the *real* Identity shines forth. Then the superimposed self disappears, the way a wrong conviction disappears when it is seen to be unfounded in truth.

And yet, even after the realization of the eternal Self, there persists the stubborn habits of thought and the convincing sense of bodily separateness and individuality; and so the duality of Self and soul continues to exist. However, the knowledge of the Self, once revealed, dissolves the foundation for belief in a separate identity, and continually erodes the self-centered habits that

condition the ego-mind. The will and paramount desire of
the projected self becomes the will and desire of the true
Self; i.e., becomes universal and divine Love. Disillusioned,
and no longer interested in separative attainments once it
has known its own universality, the self has no other will or
desire than the extollment of Truth for the joy and
disillusionment of all beings.

Frequently, the clear realization dawns within me that
there are not two, but only I AM. And at such times I
embrace the non-dualistic attitude expounded by the
jnanis. At other times, I am the humble servant of God,
trembling in His Light, asking only to fulfill the service I
have pledged to my merciful and gracious Lord. These two
paths, though they seem so contrary one to the other, are
both necessary and true from their own perspectives. The
unitive view is, of course, the truth, the final and only
Truth. And yet, the world-illusion has its own sort of
reality, as it is produced by God, and the appearance of a
separate identity also has its own ephemeral reality by
God's design.

To say, "I am God," as Mansur al-Hallaj did, is offensive
to the *bhakta,* for it denies the separate existence and
fallibility of the individual soul; and to say, "I am the servant
of God," does not satisfy the *jnani,* for it asserts a duality
where none in fact exists. I am convinced that, if we are to
speak truly and to live realistically, it is necessary to
embrace *both* attitudes, and to relinquish the logic which
begs for an either/or approach to identity. The greatest
contemplatives who've ever lived, having pondered this
quandary, have come to the same conclusion, and have
taken a position which defies categorization into one classi-
fication or another.

The best example I know is that of Jesus of Nazareth.
He had realized his true, eternal, Self; and had exclaimed, "I
and the Father are one." And yet he taught his disciples to
pray to "Our Father, who art in heaven." He embraced
both his eternal Identity and his earthly creature identity.
At times he identified with the eternal Self, and at other
times he adopted the role of suppliant to God, and advised
his disciples to do likewise. To his close disciples he taught
the truth that, "You are the Light of the world." But he
knew that few could understand the fact that man's true
Self is identical with God, and that many would react
angrily to such a saying. So he said to his disciples, "If they
ask you, 'Are you It?', say, 'We are Its children; we are the
elect of the living Father.'"

Another example is the Blessed Jan Ruysbroeck, a 14th
century disciple of Meister Eckhart, who wrote:

> Though I have said before that we are one with
> God, ... yet now I will say that we must eternally remain
> other than God, and distinct from Him. ... And we must
> understand and feel *both* within us, if all is to be right
> with us. [3]

Because the path of love and the path of knowledge are
equally valid, it is posssible to love God while being at the
same time aware that God is the all-pervading Reality
which includes one's own self. In the following song of that
famous 15th century poet-saint of India, the incomparable
Kabir, we can hear that perfect blending of the devotion of
the *bhakta* and the unitive knowledge of the *jnani*:

> O brothers, the love of God is sweet!
> Wherever I go, I offer salutations to the Lord;

Whatever I do is an act of worship to Him.
In sleep, I reverence Him; I bow my knee to no other.
Whatever I utter is His Name;
Whatever I hear reminds me of Him.
Whatever I eat or drink is to His honor.
To me, society and solitude are one,
For all feelings of duality have left me.
I have no need to practice austerity,
For I see Him smiling everywhere
As the supreme Beauty in every form.
Whether sitting, walking or performing actions,
My heart remains pure, for my mind remains fixed on God.
Says Kabir: "I have experienced the divine state
Beyond joy and suffering, and I am absorbed in That."
O brothers, the love of God is sweet! [4]

The great Maharashtran saint, Jnaneshvar, also spoke
of this blending of knowledge and devotion. Seven hundred
years ago, when he was but a youth, he spoke eloquently of
the spontaneous love of God that arises even in the hearts
of the enlightened. He called this "natural devotion." His
poetic expression of this wisdom, from the 9th chapter of
his *Amritanubhav* called "The Secret Of Natural
Devotion," is unsurpassable:

Just as a nose might become a fragrance, or ears
might give out a melody for their own enjoyment, or the
eyes might produce a mirror in order to see themselves;
... just so, the one pure Consciousness becomes the
enjoyer and the object of enjoyment, the seer and the
object of vision, without disturbing its unity.
... One may purchase a necklace, earrings, or a
bracelet -- but it is only gold, whichever one receives.
One may gather a handful of ripples -- but it is only
water in the hand. ... Likewise, the sensible universe is

only the vibration of the Self. ... There is really no action
or inaction; everything that is happening is the sport of
the Self.

The undivided One enters the courtyard of duality
of His own accord. Unity only becomes strengthened by
the expansion of diversity. Sweeter even than the bliss
of liberation is the enjoyment of sense objects to one who
has attained wisdom. In the house of *bhakti* (devotion)
that lover and his God experience their sweet union.

... God Himself is the devotee; the goal is the path.
The whole universe is one solitary Being. It is He who
becomes a God, and He who becomes a devotee. In
Himself, He enjoys the kingdom of Stillness. ...
Everything is contained in the Being of God. ... If a desire
for the Master-disciple relationship arises, it is God
alone who must supply both out of Himself.

Even the devotional practices, such as *japa*
(repetition of God's name), faith and meditation, are not
different from God. Therefore, God must worship God
with God, in one way or another. The temple, the idol,
and the priests -- all are carved out of the same stone
mountain. Why, then should there be devotional
worship? [Why should there *not* be devotional
worship?] A tree spreads its foliage, and produces
flowers and fruits, even though it has no objective
outside of itself.

... A wise person is aware that he, himself, is the
Lord, Shiva; therefore, even when he is not worshipping,
he is worshipping. No matter where he goes, that sage is
making pilgrimage to Shiva. And if he attains to Shiva,
that attainment is non-attainment. ... No matter what his
eyes fall upon at any time, he always enjoys the vision of
Shiva. If Shiva Himself appears before him, it is as if he
has seen nothing; for God and His devotee are on the
same level.

... This spontaneous, natural devotion cannot be
touched by the hand of action, nor can knowledge

> penetrate it. It goes on without end, in communion with
> itself. What bliss can be compared to this? This natural
> devotion is a wonderful secret. It is the place in which
> meditation and knowledge become merged.
>   ... O blissful and almighty Lord! You have made us
> the sole sovereign in the kingdom of perfect Bliss. ... We
> are Yours entirely. Out of love, You include us as Your
> own, as is befitting Your greatness. ... Would the
> scriptures have extolled You, if, by sharing it with Your
> devotee, Your unity were disturbed? O noble One! It is
> Your pleasure to become our nearest and dearest by
> taking away from us our sense of difference from You. [5]

Just as the Self and the soul cannot be separated one
from the other, neither can *jnan* and *bhakti* be separated;
though mutually exclusive, they co-exist as complements in
everyone. And as our knowledge grows, we must learn to
adapt our vision of the world to accept and embrace
apparently contradictory views. We must learn to feel
comfortable with the notion that a quantity of energy is
both a wave *and* a particle; that our lives are determined,
and that we are free; that our identity is both the Whole
and the part. We are the universal Self; we *are* the one
Consciousness -- and we are also the individualized soul
which consists of the mind and its own private impressions.
We are the Ocean -- but we are also the wave.

We are *Shiva*, but we are also *Shakti*. We are perfect,
but we are also imperfect. We are the eternal Reality, but
we are also the ephemeral image It projects on Its own
screen. We are indeed the Dreamer, but we are also the
dream. We are entitled to say, "I am *Shiva*," but so long as
the Shakti-mind exists, it must sing the song of love and
devotion to its Lord. While we live and move in this
phantasmagoria, we are His creatures, and are utterly

dependent upon His grace. Therefore, if we truly understand our own double-faceted reality, we must learn to sing two songs: one, the song of Love; the other, the song of our own immortal Self. Neither, without the other, is complete.

THE SONG OF LOVE

Thou art Love, and I shall follow all Thy ways.
I shall have no care, for Love cares only to love.
I shall have no fear, for Love is fearless;
Nor shall I frighten any,
For Love comes sweetly and meek.
I shall keep no violence within me,
Neither in thought nor in deed,
For Love comes peacefully.
I shall bear no shield or sword,
For the defense of Love is love.
I shall seek Thee in the eyes of men,
For love seeks Thee always.
I shall keep silence before Thine enemies,
And lift to them Thy countenance,
For all are powerless before Thee.
I shall keep Thee in my heart with precious care,
Lest Thy light be extinguished by the winds;
For without Thy light, I am in darkness.
I shall go free in the world with Thee --
Free of all bondage to anything but Thee --
For Thou art my God, the sole Father of my being,
The sweet breath of Love that lives in my heart;
And I shall follow Thee, and live with Thee,
And lean on Thee till the end of my days.

THE SONG OF THE SELF

O my God, even this body is Thine own!
Though I call to Thee and seek Thee amidst chaos,
Even I who seemed an unclean pitcher amidst Thy
    waters --
Even I am Thine own.

Does a wave cease to be of the ocean?
Do the mountains and the gulfs cease to be of the
    earth?
Or does a pebble cease to be stone?
How can I escape Thee?
Thou art even That which thinks of escape!

Even now, I speak the word, "Thou,"and create
    duality.
I love, and create hatred.
I am in peace, and am fashioning chaos.
Standing on the peak, I necessitate the depths.
But now, weeping and laughing are gone;
Night is become day.

Music and silence are heard as one;
My ears are all the universe.

All motion has ceased; everything continues.
Life and death no longer stand apart.
No I, no Thou;

No now, or then.
Unless I move, there is no stillness.

Nothing to lament, nothing to vanquish,
Nothing to pride oneself on;
All is accomplished in an instant.
All may now be told without effort.
Where is there a question?
Where is the temple?
Which the Imperishable, which the abode?

I am the pulse of the turtle;
I am the clanging bells of joy.
I bring the dust of blindness;
I am the fire of song.
I am in the clouds and in the gritty soil;
In pools of clear water my image is found.

I am the dust on the feet of the wretched,
The toothless beggars of every land.
I have given sweets that decay to those who crave
     them;
I have given my wealth unto the poor and lonely.
My hands are open -- nothing is concealed.

All things move together of one accord;
Assent is given throughout the universe to every
     falling grain.
The Sun stirs the waters of my heart,
And the vapor of my love flies to the four corners of
     the world;

The Moon stills me, and the cold darkness is my
   bed.

I have but breathed, and everything is rearranged
And set in order once again.
A million worlds begin and end in every breath,
And, in this breathing, all things are sustained.

2. THE ULTIMATE UNITY

Even today, over thirty years later, I experience that
same alternation between Unity and duality, between *jnan*
and *bhakti*. There are times when the recognition of my
own Self as the ultimate Reality bestows profound inner joy.
My own consciousness becomes free of thought; and
supreme peace, bell-like clarity, and an imperturbable
happiness fills my whole being. The sound of my own
breath becomes the mantra, *So-ham*, "I am That"; and my
mind is bathed in the calm certain awareness of my eternal
Identity.

Then, unexpectedly, the heart speaks, and once again
duality raises its head. The image addresses the Imager;
the projected soul, feeling powerless, reaches toward its
governing Source, and the love of God is born anew. It is
born of that inherent tendency in the unitive Divinity
toward Self-division, toward the dualistic play of subject and
object, of 'I' and 'Thou'.

At such times my heart is flooded with gratitude to my
Lord, my God, and thrills rush through my body and my
soul, causing tears of love to cascade down my cheeks.
Such love of God is truly the awareness of my greater Self,
and I am overcome by the fervent desire to praise Him and
to express my love -- even though I know that this poor
mind is only pretending to be separate, and its babbling is
only God's grace expressing its own love in me. The soul
loves, but it is His Love that carries on the play of lover and
Beloved. He himself is the sweet song of love that sings in
my heart.

Such alternation between *bhakti* and *jnan* will ever continue. It is not a product of indecisiveness, but is a product of the complementary nature of Reality. For we live simultaneously in two frameworks of reality: that of the divisible world of multiple phenomena, and that of the eternal Self, the unbroken Whole. All the great issues and arguments of science, philosophy and theology are solved in one stroke by the understanding of this dual-sidedness of reality. From the standpoint of my *Shakti*-identity, my life in the universal drama is fixed and determined. From the standpoint of my *Shiva*-identity, as the eternal witness, I am ever free.

When I identify myself as *Shakti*, I am an individual soul guided by the hand of God; and the planetary configurations relating to my position on earth strongly affect my mental, emotional and physical being. When I identify myself as *Shiva*, I am the one all-pervading Soul of the universe; I am the Cause of all, the One in whom the stars and planets exist, and I remain unaffected by the changes taking place within the manifested world.

When I identify myself as *Shakti*, I am *Shiva's* servant; I worship Him as my Lord, and I am surrendered to His will. When I identify myself as *Shiva*, there are not two, but only one -- and I am that One. These two identities are not a hair's breadth apart; for the one is superimposed upon the other. Our separative identity and our infinite Identity, the wave and the Ocean, are complementary aspects of the same one Reality.

God is always accessible to us as our own Self. We have only to quiet the mind to become aware of our eternal Identity. And even when we are active in the world we are continually in His presence. If we can refine our vision, and become aware of the dual-sidedness of our own nature, we will then be able to see that not only are we the Self, but everything around us is also the Self. The subject is the Self; the object is the Self. Truly, no matter who or what I see or speak to, it is really only my own Self. If we could really grasp the truth of this, what a revolution would occur in our thinking and behavior!

Just as waves on the ocean are only water, just as golden ornaments are only gold, so all the various forms in the universe are forms of our own Self. Becoming aware of this, we would begin to revel in that joy which had been missing in our lives before. We would begin to drink the nectar of the unending Love for which we had been thirsting before. And we would begin to take delight in just being and living and acting in the world in a way we had been unable to before. The universal division into respective subjects and objects does not cease; the world goes on, even for the enlightened. It is just that she *knows* in her heart, with an indomitable certainty, that she and the universe are one.

Just as a chess-player retains the awareness that the antagonism between him and his opponent is merely a temporary game of role-playing, and that, at the end of the game, both the red and the black pieces will be thrown into the same box -- in the same way, one who has clearly experienced the unbroken Whole retains the knowledge of the ultimate Unity, and sees the play of subjects and objects as the ongoing pretense or play of the one Self.

This is why, after more than thirty years since His revelation to me, I cannot forget Him: He is always in my thoughts; His name is sounded in my mind at every moment, and I see Him around me in every form, in every activity. When I walk, I walk in His presence in great gladness; when I sit, I sit in the awareness that all is perfect, all is His glorious play. I play out the role He has given me to play, and I watch Him in all His other forms playing out the roles destined for those souls: the mother, the businesss-man, the sports hero, the physicist, the druggist, the doctor, the artist.

Each soul is limited by its role; none can be all things, but each must accept the limitation required for success in the performance of its own purpose. And all are but that one bright Consciousness masquerading as individual souls. All is God; there is nothing here that is not Him. Listen, once more, to Jnaneshvar:

> There is nothing else here but the Self. Whether appearing as the *seen* or perceiving as the *seer*, nothing else exists besides the Self. ... Just as water plays with itself by assuming the forms of waves, the Self, the ultimate reality, plays happily with Himself. Though there are multitudes of visible objects, and wave upon wave of mental images, still they are not different from their witness. You may break a lump of raw sugar into a million pieces, still there is nothing but sugar. Likewise, the unity of the Self is not lost, even though He fills the whole universe. He is seeing only His own Self -- like one who discovers various countries in his imagination, and goes wandering through them all with great enjoyment.[6]

3.   DEVOTION AND GRACE

Just as there are many religious devotees (*bhaktas*) who refuse to acknowledge man's supreme Identity as God, the one transcendent Self, there are also many philosophical Monists (*jnanis*) who refuse to open their hearts to the Love of God, protesting that the fact of unity precludes such an attitude, and that the preservation of an "I-Thou" relationship only prolongs the delusion of duality. I would like to point out to such people that so long as we are not lifted into the experience of unity by the grace of God, duality continues to exist for us -- whether we admit to it or not. The grace of God is an experience of Love, a Love that draws us to the experience of unity. Without it, we can never know God as our supreme Self.

The Love of God is not a love between a subject and an object; for in this case, the subject, the object, and the Love itself, are one. Nor is this Love the result of a conclusion based on a rational premise; it is an inner experience. It is something quite real -- breathtakingly and intoxicatingly real. It stirs from within, and centers on itself within. It is not a thought-out construction based on philosophical reasoning, but a sweetness that is itself the object of devotion. It is this Love that *bhaktas* love. It has no location but the human heart, yet its source is the universal Being. It is His gracious gift, and only those who have experienced it know what it is.

It is of this Love that Sri Ramakrishna sang:

How are you trying, O my mind, to know the nature of God?
You are groping like a madman locked in a dark room.

He is grasped through ecstatic love;
How can you fathom Him without it?
When that Love awakes, the Lord,
Like a magnet, draws to Him the soul. [7]

Such love-longing for God always precedes the experience of enlightenment because it is the natural expression, the indicator, of a shift in the consciousness toward the transcendent Unity. All of the outer events as well as the inner ones will conspire to bring one's life to that point where enlightenment is experienced. When it is time for it to come, it will produce itself, and it will announce its coming by a great wave of love that steers the heart irresistably to the source of that Love, and eventually reveals itself unaided from within.

Consider the great Shankaracharya's final message to the disciple in his *Vivekachudamani:*

Gurus and scriptures can stimulate spiritual awareness, but one crosses the ocean of ignorance only by
direct illumination, *through the grace of God.* [8]

No one has ever realized God except those to whom He has revealed Himself. On this point all Self-realized beings are unanimously agreed. As one commentator says, in the Tantric text, *Malini Vijaya Vartika:* "The learned men of all times always hold that the descent of grace does not have any cause or condition, but depends entirely on the free will of the Lord." The case may be made, of course, that "grace" is the subjective reading of the influence of the planetary patterns evolving into effect at the time, and not a spur-of-the-moment volitional act by a supreme Being. But, we must object, is not the supreme Cause guiding the unfoldment of the evolving universe? Do not all things move together of (His) one accord? And is He not, therefore, ultimately responsible for every single event in this universe, including the movements of the planets, and man's ultimate realization of his eternal Identity?

Another Tantric scripture, the *Tantraloka*, states:

> Divine grace leads the individual to the path of spiritual realization. It is the only cause of Self-realization and is independent of human effort. [9]

What is grace, then, but God's unconditional gift, given of His own free will? Were it dependent upon conditions, it would not be absolute and independent grace. What, indeed, in all this universe of phenomena, could be considered apart from His grace? Can we imagine that His highest gift, His realization, is an accident outside of His doing? No.

The experience of Self-realization occurs when the mind is concentrated to a fine laser-point and focused in contemplation of God; but this happens only by the power of the universal Self, of God Himself. This is not a denial of the efficacy of self-effort, but merely an assertion that every effort or desire to remember Him, every intensification of concentration on Him, is instigated by Himself, for He is our own inner Self, the inner Controller. It is He who inspires, enacts, and consummates all our efforts. If the planetary patterns also reflect the arising of divine Consciousness, and the dawn of mystical experience in our lives, that is merely additional evidence that "all things move together of one accord," that He is indeed the Lord of the universe.

Among the Christian mystics, we find complete agreement on this issue; Saint Bernard of Clairvaux, for example, says: "You would not seek Him at all, O soul, nor love Him at all, if you had not been first sought and first loved."[10] And Meister Eckhart acknowledges: "It is He that prays in us and not we ourselves." [11]   The Blessed Jan Ruysbroeck concurs:

> Contemplation places us in a purity and radiance which is far above our understanding, ... and no one can attain to it by knowledge, by subtlety, or by any exercise whatsoever; but he whom God chooses to unite to Himself, and to illumine by Himself, he and no other can contemplate God. [12]

We find the same agreement among the Sufi mystics, the Hindus and the Buddhists. It is always so -- always. And though the attempt is often made by charlatans to translate the description of the mental state of the mystic at the time of his experience of unity into a sort of 'method' or 'scientific technique' for the attainment of God, no one has ever claimed that the following of such a technique has actually produced the advertised result. For, by themselves, the practices of shallow breathing, fixed stares, and cessation of thought, will never produce the experience of unity. This experience comes only by the Will of God. Nanak, the great founder of the Sikh tradition, acknowledging this truth, wrote:

> Liberation from bondage depends upon Thy Will; there is no one to gainsay it. Should a fool wish to, suffering will teach him wisdom. [13]

An even more telling remark is made by Dadu, a
mystic-poet who lived shortly after Nanak, and who, like
him, eschewed both Islamic and Hindu religious traditions:

> Omniscient God, it is by Thy grace alone that I have
> been blessed with vision of Thee.
> Thou knowest all; what can I say?
> All-knowing God, I can conceal nothing from Thee.
> I have nothing that deserves Thy grace.
> No one can reach Thee by his own efforts; Thou
> showest Thyself by Thine own grace.
> How could I approach Thy presence? By what
> means could I gain Thy favor?
> And by what powers of mind or body could I attain to
> Thee?
> It hath pleased Thee in Thy mercy to take me under
> Thy wing.
> Thou alone art the Beginning and the End; Thou art
> the Creator of the three worlds.
> Dadu says: I am nothing and can do nothing.
> Truly, even a fool may reach Thee by Thy grace. [14]

The desire for God is a very special grace, not given to
all. When that desire arises, it fires the heart and fills the
mind, just as other desires -- such as the desire for a wife,
children and other worldly objects --possess the minds of so
many. And just as those desires precede and give impetus
to their fulfillment, so does the desire for God precede the
fulfillment of that desire, resulting in the soul's experience
of union with God.

When He draws the mind to Himself, the mind
becomes still automatically. It is not necessary to attempt
to still the mind by austere practices or artificial methods.
The body becomes still, the mind becomes still when the

heart is yearning sincerely for Him alone. Everything happens very naturally by His grace. One begins to begrudge the mind any thought save the thought directed to God. And with the aim of centering the mind continually on Him, one begins to sing His name in the inner recesses of the mind.

It doesn't matter what name is used; Christians call Him, "Father," Muslims call Him "Rahim," Jews call Him "Adonai," and Hindus call Him "Hari"; Love responds to whatever name is called with love. To one who loves, His name is nectar; it is like a cold drink of water to a thirsty man. It is no discipline, nor is it an austerity. It is the living of a joyful life. It is the sweetness of peace; it is the delight of delights.

Since there is really nothing else but that infinite Being wherever one may look, as one begins to sing the name of God, that awareness dawns, and the bliss of recognizing one's own Self both without and within begins to well up. The more one sings His name, the more one revels in that bliss, and the more clearly one perceives His continual presence. Inherent in that perception is all mercy, all right-judgement, all tenderness, all loving-kindness. It is the *natural devotion* by which a man's heart is transformed, and by which he becomes fit for the vision of God.

It seems that everyone, sooner or later, in this life or the next, comes to experience the grace of God. It is experienced as an 'awakening of the soul,' a prerequisite to the direct knowledge of God, one's eternal Self. This 'awakening' very often coincides with the hearing or reading of the words of someone who has had an intimate experience of the Self, and who is able to communicate the understanding he or she has acquired. It is in this way, through our intellects, that God reaches to our hearts.

Speaking from my own experience, the moment I learned of the ultimate identity of man's self and the universal Self, and of the fact that many have actually experienced this truth, a delicious joy arose in me coupled with a certainty that it was indeed true. I *felt* that inner grace; I knew that I had found the truth of existence, and I rejoiced in that blissful knowledge! This, I believe, is a common experience, a universal symptom of the first flush of the soul's awakening to the Self.

Sometimes this awakening is accompanied by thrills of joy that run up the spine into the head. Sometimes there are interior visions, either of saints or temples or simply of a golden light. But it is unmistakeable; it is truly an awakening of the soul, and is known and experienced as such.

One can be sure that, at such a time, the planetary progressions and transits are relating to one's natal planetary configurations in a unique, though temporary, manner, involving in most cases the placement of planets in prominent and significant relationship to the natal position of Neptune. Such events, both cosmic and mundane, happen rarely in the course of a life, and signal a transient period of increased sensitivity to the spiritual reality in which we live. It is clear that, as our destinies unfold, as the heavens tell the passing of our days, the focus of our awareness undergoes gradual changes. A decade ago, we sought quite different goals from those which we seek at present; and yet different objectives motivated us ten years before that. These changes occur so gradually that we scarcely notice that we have changed; yet each

new era in the unfolding of our destiny has its own focus, its
own learning experiences.

Eventually, each of us passes through a specific period
in our lives during which our understanding is awakened to
the eternal Self, when we are most keenly receptive to the
awareness of God's presence and Love. Years later, our
ability to experience that same sense of God's presence and
Love may wane; perhaps we shall pass into a period of more
mundane considerations during which we will learn to carry
the understandings which we gained in those more ecstatic
and spiritually receptive moments into our daily lives, and to
remain obedient to that acquired wisdom. There is, as the
author of *Ecclesiastes* tells us, to everything a season, and a
time to every purpose under heaven; a time for sowing, and
a time for reaping, a time for giving, and a time for
receiving.

The point I wish to make is that the time of peak
receptivity, the time of grace, is short; and should be
cherished and utilized with care. Once that unmistakeable awakening has occurred, find some time to enjoy
a period of solitude with God. You will learn more in such
moments than in a thousand congregational lectures.
Forge your link with God, and He will lead you to Himself.
He will draw you to love Him, for He Himself is that Love
that has awakened in you as love for God. He will draw you
to seek Him in prayer and in silent longing, for He is your
own heart. Follow, and you will reach Him. Draw near to
Him in the silence of the night and He will reveal Himself
to you as your very deepest Self, your eternal Identity.

There are some who feel the need to follow closely in
the shadow of some great spiritually aware personage in
order to learn how to live in harmony with their own

Divinity; but they should be wary of surrendering their own innate intelligence in service to another, however holy he or she may seem. Teachers are often necessary, and their Divinity is worthy of honor; but dependence on another is full of danger, and is to be avoided. Depend upon God; it is *His* grace you seek, and the awakening of Love within your own heart. *That* is the only fee for entrance into the kingdom of God.

Keep on loving Him, keep on trusting in Him to guide you, and keep on praying to Him. And when He puts it into your heart to know Him, He will lift aside the veil, and reveal that, all along, it was *He* who prayed, who sought, who sorrowed as you; and that, all along, it was *you* who forever lives beyond all sorrow, as God -- forever blissful, forever free.

∞∞

APPENDIX

This Appendix is added for the benefit of those who have some familiarity with astrological principles and are able to understand the significance of the following charts:

The first chart, chart A, is the chart of the *transitting* planetary arrangement in effect at the time of my "experience of unity." The lines connecting those planets in *opposition* (180º) *trine* (120º), and *sextile* (60º) aspects to each other show the angular relationships between these transitting planets. This, in itself, is a remarkable configuration. But to fully appreciate the significance of this transitting planetary arrangement, it must be seen in relationship to the positions of the planets at my birth.

This may be seen in chart B. It is a composite chart, showing the positions of the planets in my natal, progressed, and transitting charts, shown in consecutive wheels. In the center wheel, my *natal* chart, calculated for 6:01 P.M., August 14, 1938, at Indianapolis, Indiana; in the intermediate wheel, my *progressed* chart for 9:00 P.M., November 18, 1966, at Santa Cruz, California; and in the outer wheel, the *transitting* chart for the same time and place.

CHART A

Nov 18 1966   9:00 PM PST
Santa Cruz   California
38N00   121W53
Nov 19 1966   05:00:00 GMT
Tropical   **Placidus**   **True Node**

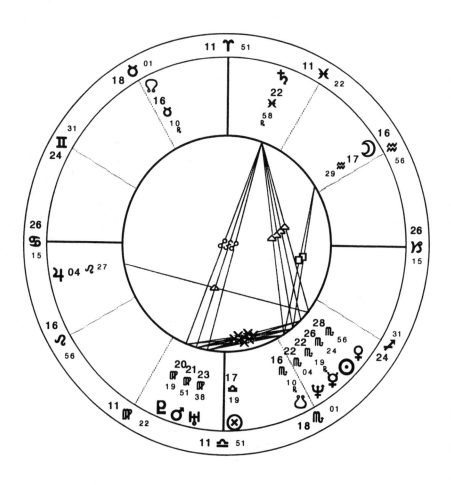

CHART B

Stan Trout
Aug 14 1938   6:01 PM CST
Indianapolis   Indiana
39N46   86W09
Aug 15 1938   00:01:00 GMT
Tropical   Placidus   True Node

Second Chart   Solar Arc Progression
Stan Trout SAP
Nov 19 1966   05:00:00 GMT
Third Chart
Stan TroutTrans.
Nov 19 1966   05:00:00 GMT

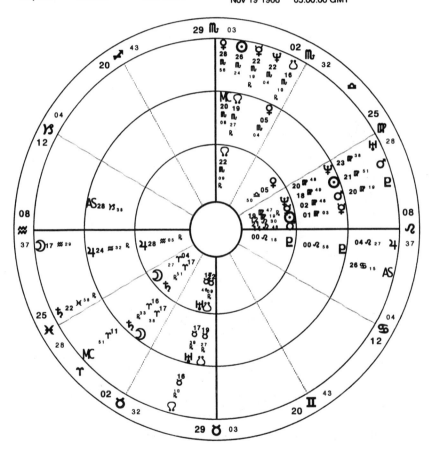

Natal Aspects:
   Sun conjunct Mars
   Sun trine Saturn
   Sun square Uranus
   Mercury trine Uranus
   Mercury conjunct Neptune
   Mars square Uranus
   Saturn semisextile Uranus
   Uranus trine Neptune

Progressed Aspects (to natal planets):
   Moon conjunct Saturn (exact)
   Moon semisextile Uranus (exact)
   Sun conjunct Neptune (exact)

Transitting Aspects (to natal planets):
   Moon sextile Saturn (exact)
   Moon square Uranus (exact)
   Sun conjunct Midheaven
   Mercury square Sun (exact)
   Mercury conjunct North Node (exact)
   Venus conjunct Midheaven (exact)
   Venus square Jupiter (exact)
   Mars conjunct Neptune
   Jupiter trine Moon (exact)
   Uranus conjunct Neptune
   Neptune conjunct North Node (exact)
   Neptune square Sun (exact)
   Pluto conjunct Neptune (exact)

Note: planets within 1º aspect are considered to be exact.

In examining this composite of charts, the first thing
that stands out to the trained eye is the highly significant
progression of both the Sun and the Moon (middle wheel) to
exact conjunctions with natal planets (center wheel). The
Moon's progression to an exact conjunction to my natal
Saturn is a conjunction which occurs only once every
twenty-eight to thirty years; while the Sun's progression to
the natal position of Neptune occurs in one's chart only if
one's Sun position is natally within 60° or so, clockwise, of
Neptune's position -- and then, only once in a lifetime. The
likelihood of both the Sun and Moon forming progressed
conjunctions to (major) natal planets simultaneously is
obviously very remote, and when it *does* occur, is highly
significant of an extraordinary event.

Neptune, to which the progressed Sun is conjoined,
figures quite prominently in my natal chart, as it forms
there a conjunction to Mercury and a trine to Uranus. In
my early deliberations about my own chart, I had come to
look on it as a representation of a certain mental receptivity
to poetic inspiration. But Neptune represents much more
than that; with beneficial aspects from other planets it can
represent an access to the very subtlest of spiritual realms.
One astrologer, Robert Hand, who is a recognized authority
on astrological symbols, says about Neptune:

> Neptune symbolizes the truth and divinity perceived
> by mystics. (*Keep in mind that the planet is an agent
> or a representation of an energy, not the source of
> the energy.*) At the highest level, Neptune represents
> Nirvana, where all individuality is merged into an infinite
> oneness of being and consciousness. [6]

Notice that the massive conjunction of transitting Mars-Uranus-Pluto (outer wheel) is precisely over my natal Neptune, along with the progressed Sun, and that the conjunction of transitting Mercury-Neptune is precisely over my natal North Node of the Moon. There were, on that night of November 18, 1966, two exact conjunctions of *progressed* planets to natal planets, and ten exact aspects of *transitting* planets to natal positions, five of which were conjunctions. The concentration of energy over my natal Neptune position was clearly intense -- intense enough for even a thick-headed person like myself to catch a glimpse of God.

If it could be shown that, in all cases, the mystical experience of Unity coincided with progressed solar and/or lunar aspects to Neptune in the charts of the experiencers, we would be in possession of a neatly consistent formula for anticipating mystical experience. However, that does not seem always to be the case. When one examines the charts of known mystics of the past progressed to the date of their transcendent experience, one encounters a very inconsistent collection of varied influences, although aspects to the natal Neptune position do seem to figure strongly.

For example, in the chart of Sri Aurobindo (born August 15, 1872), at the time of his reported enlightenment (January 15, 1908) the progressed moon is exactly conjunct his natal Neptune, and the progressed Sun is exactly quincunx Neptune's position. In the chart of Sri Ramakrishna (born February 18, 1836), progressed to the date of his first *samadhi* at the age of twenty-nine (February 1, 1865), the progressed moon is exactly sextile his natal Neptune's position, while there are no major aspects from the progressed Sun. And in the progressed chart of Sri Ramana Maharshi (born December 30, 1879), who became enlightened at the age of sixteen (September 15, 1896), the progressed moon is 3º past a conjunction with natal Jupiter, and the progressed Sun makes only one aspect: a trine to natal Pluto. Even with so brief a sampling, it is clear that there is a wide range of variation in the progressed solar and lunar aspects occurring at the time of enlightenment.

Strangely enough, the one modern mystic whose progressed aspects at the time of his enlightenment most closely resemble the planetary aspects present in my own enlightenment chart is someone who was personally known to me -- Swami Muktananda. I met Swami Muktananda in 1970 when he gave a Talk at the University of California at Santa Cruz during his first World Tour. After his return to Ganeshpuri, India, where his ashram was located, I also journeyed there to live and practice meditation under his tutelege. It was Muktananda who served as my guru for ten years, and who, in 1978, initiated me into *sannyas,* and gave me the name I presently bear.

Swami Muktananda (1908-1982) had been a wandering *sadhu* in India since his early teens, had lived in the ashrams of various teachers and had met many saints and holy men, but he had not met his spiritual master until he was initiated by Bhagavan Nityananda in 1947. Nityananda was a great and powerful yogi who had wandered naked most of his life, meditating for long periods of time in caves and wildernesses, and who had finally settled in Ganeshpuri, about 30 miles north of Bombay, where a small village and the ashram of Swami Muktananda now exists.

Nityananda had been known as an *avadhut*, a renunciant who had no more worldly attachment left, and who was free as the wind, wandering with no house, no clothes, taking food as it came to him. He was recognized to have had enormous yogic powers; and near the time of his death in 1961, he had transferred his immense power to Muktananda, and Muktananda carried on the tradition in the lineage of Siddhas -- perfect masters. Earlier, Muktananda had been sent by his guru into a prolonged period of *sadhana*, or spiritual retreat, and after years of solitary meditation, during which time he went through many amazing and wonderful inner experiences, eventually became Self-realized at the age of forty-nine, through the grace of God and his guru.

Muktananda's natal horoscope reveals him to have been an immensely powerful personality, but it only hints at the tremendous personal power he came to possess through the legacy of *shaktipat* transmitted to him by his guru, Nityananda, and through his lifelong retention of that power. He was totally unique in his masterful attainment, and his life of sharing his spiritual realizations was also amazing and unique; but *his experience of the Self was the common experience of all the enlightened.*

While our paths to enlightenment, our visions, our circumstances, personalities and destinies (as symbolized in our individual horoscopes) were very different, the enlightenment experience which revealed the eternal Self to Muktananda was identical (by definition) with that which I experienced. What's more, the planetary significators of enlightenment were nearly identical in both our cases.

Despite the unique elements of Muktananda's *sadhana,* which differed considerably from my own experience, both of our actual enlightenment experiences, though nearly ten years apart, coincided with a strong aspect of the progressed moon to one of the outer natal planets, at the same time that *the progressed Sun was forming an exact conjunction with the natal position of Neptune.* There was also, at the time, an extraordinary and significant array of transitting planets in the heavens in both cases. Here is a chart showing the positions of the transitting planets on the day of Muktananda's enlightenment (determined to be July 30, 1957):

Jul 30 1957   11:00 PM INT
Yeola   India
19N00   72E50
Jul 30 1957   17:30:00 GMT
Tropical   Placidus   True Node

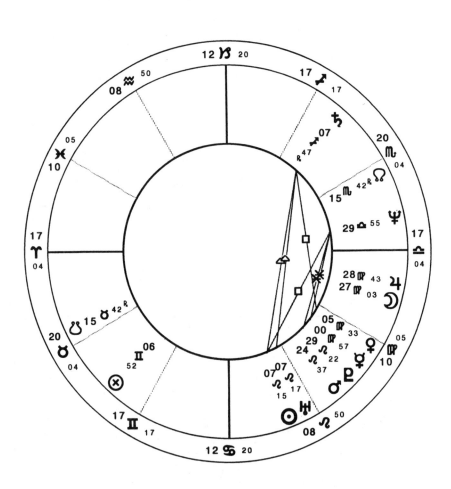

And here is a composite chart for the time of Muktananda's enlightenment (the inner wheel is his natal chart; the middle wheel is the progressed chart; and the outer wheel represents the transiting positions of the planets on that day):

Swami Muktananda

May 16 1908	6:00 AM INT
Mangalore	India
12N52	74E53
May 16 1908	00:30:00 GMT
Tropical	Placidus	True Node

Second Chart   Solar Arc Progression
Swami Muktananda SAP
Jul 30 1957   17:30 GMT

Third Chart
S. M. Transit7-30-57
Jul 30 1957   17:30:00 GMT

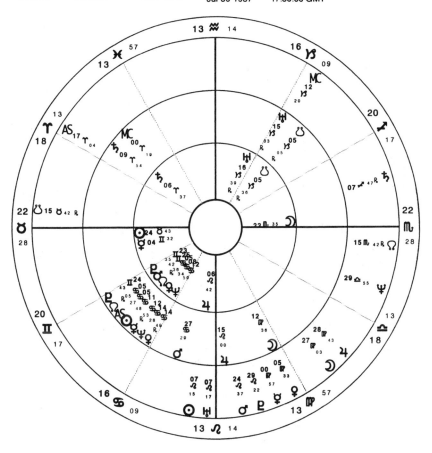

Natal Aspects:

Sun conjunct Ascendant
Sun opposite moon
Mercury sextile Jupiter
Venus conjunct Neptune
Venus square Saturn
Mars conjunct Pluto
Jupiter trine Saturn (exact)
Uranus opposite Neptune

Progressed Aspects (to natal planets):

Sun-Mercury conjunct Neptune (exact)
Moon sextile Neptune (exact)
Jupiter quincunx Uranus

Transitting Aspects (to natal planets):

Sun-Uranus conjunct Jupiter
Sun-Uranus trine Saturn
Moon-Jupiter trine Sun (moon exact)
Mars-Pluto square Sun
Saturn trine Jupiter
Saturn trine Saturn

Note: Planets within 1º aspect are considered to be exact.

In Muktananda's *natal* chart, notice the powerful stellium of planets in the 2nd House, along with the Sun-moon opposition closely conjunct the 1st-7th House cusps. Mars conjunct Pluto, and Venus conjunct Neptune give some indication of his spiritual evolution and the great forcefulness of his personal energy. Jupiter in the 3rd House shows his learning and speaking ability, and Uranus on the 9th House cusp relates both to his advanced philosophical views and his amazingly broad travels. (For a thoughtful and thorough examination of his life from an astrological point of view, see the excellent treatment by my good friend, Greg Bogart, in his book, *Astrology And Spiritual Awakening,* published by Dawn Mountain Press.)

The *progressed* chart shows the progressed Sun and Mercury in exact conjunction with his natal Neptune, and the progressed Moon in exact sextile to natal Neptune. In addition to these highly significant aspects, Jupiter is progressed to an exact quincunx to natal Uranus.

The *transitting* aspects are equally notable: a transitting Sun-Uranus conjunction is conjunct natal Jupiter, trining natal Saturn, while transitting Saturn is forming a grand trine with natal Saturn and Jupiter. A transitting Moon-Jupiter conjunction is trining the natal Sun, while transitting Mars, Pluto, and Mercury are in close square to that natal Sun position. All in all, it is a remarkable set of circumstances, signalling a remarkable occurrence. Clearly, it is *as* uniquely powerful a set of progressed and transitting aspects as those which occurred in relation to my own chart in November of 1966.

It is my opinion that this discovery of the correlation of celestial dynamics and Divine grace is a breakthrough in knowledge comparable to those brought about by Copernicus and Galileo, and has the potential to revolutionize our understanding of "spiritual" experience. However, it requires so bold a departure from traditional ways of thinking that it is unlikely to have a great influence on the understanding of any but the most discerning. In fact, many so-called 'spiritual teachers' will find this information embarrassing and will reject it, for it makes a folly of their contention that it is practices and techniques which bring about Self-realization. For without God's celestial grace, without the timing of God's heavenly motions unfolding in one's life, no illumination will come.

The present-day understanding of how astrology 'works' is as far from a comprehensive resolution as is the science of microphysics. It was a mystery to the ancients, and it is a mystery today (although the Bohmian concept of the immediate interconnectedness of everything within 'the unbroken Whole' hints at the way ahead). And while the "science" of the 'astrology of enlightenment' is in its infancy today, I am hopeful that the data that is here provided will point the way to greater exploration and understanding of the relation of astronomical phenomena to mystical experience in the years to come.

∞∞∞

About The Author

Swami Abhayananda was born Stan Trout in Indian-apolis, Indiana on August 14, 1938. After service in the Navy, he settled in northern California, where he pursued his studies in philosophy and literature. In June of 1966, he became acquainted with the philosophy of mysticism, and experienced a strong desire to realize God. Abandoning all other pursuits, he retired to a solitary life in a secluded cabin in the mountain forests near Santa Cruz, California; and, on November 18, of that same year, became enlightened by the grace of God.

He spent four more years in his isolated cabin, and subsequently met Swami Muktananda who visited Santa Cruz in 1970. Shortly thereafter, he joined Muktananda in India, as his disciple, and later lived and worked in Muktananda's Oakland, California ashram. In May of 1978, he returned to India and was initiated by his master into the ancient Order of *sannyas*, and given the monastic name, *Swami Abhayananda*, "the bliss of fearlessness."

As a Swami, he taught in various cities in the U.S., but in 1981, unwilling to condone what he saw as abuses of power, Abhayananda left Muktananda's organization, and went into retreat once again, this time for seven years, in upstate New York. It was during this time that all of his books were written, and Atma Books was founded to publish them.

At present, Swami Abhayananda is residing in the Olympia area of western Washington state, where he continues to teach, write, and publish his works on the knowledge of the Self.

NOTES

PART ONE:
THE EXPERIENCE OF THE SELF

1. *Svetasvatara Upanishad:* 6; Mascaro, Juan, 1965;
    p. 95
2. *Mundaka Upanishad:* 3.1; *Ibid.,* p. 80
3. *Katha Upanishad:* 5; *Ibid.,* p. 64
4. Plotinus, *Enneads:* VI:7.34, 36; VI: 9.5-11
5. de B. Evans, C., *Eckhart,* Vol. I., p. 221
6. Blackney, R.B., *Meister Eckhart: A Modern
    Translation;*
7. *Ibid.,* p. 206
8. Huxley, Aldous, 1944; p. 12
9. de B. Evans, C., *op. cit., Sermon XXI.*

PART TWO:
THE PHILOSOPHY OF THE SELF

1. *Rig Veda,* X.129
2. *Isha Upanishad,* 5
3. *Svetasvatara Upanishad,* 3:1; from Mascaro, 1965;
    p. 89
4. *Ibid., 4:10;* p. 93
5. *Srimad Bhagavatam,* from Prabhavananda, 1978;
    p. 5
6. *Vivekachudamani,* from Prabhavananda, 1947;
    pp. 82-84
7. *Ibid.,* pp. 58-59

8. *Ibid.,* pp.63-64
9. *Bhagavad Gita,* 14:4; based on Mascaro, Juan, 1962
10. *Ibid.,* 13:20-23
11. *Ibid.,* 13:27-34
12. *Ibid.,* 9:7-15
13. Lao Tze, *Tao Teh Ching,* 25
14. *Ibid.,* 1
15. *Ibid.,* 21
16. Chuang Tze, Ch. 22
17. Lao Tze, *Tao Teh Ching,* 52
18. *Ibid.,* 6
19. *Ibid.,* 4
20. *Ibid., 21*
21. *Ibid.,* 37
22. *Ibid.,* 51
23. *Ibid.,* 1
24. *Ibid.,* 14
25. *Ibid.,* 26
26. *Ibid.,* 28
27. *Ibid.,* 70
28. Chuang Tze, Ch. 22
29. Lao Tze, *Tao Teh Ching,* 38
30. *Ibid.,* 50
31. Chuang Tze, Ch. 22
32. *Ibid.,* Ch. 4
33. Lao Tze, *Tao Teh Ching,* 56
34. Chuang Tze, Ch. 22
35. *Avatamsaka Sutra,* from Suzuki, D.T., 1963; p. 268
36. *Ibid.,* p. 268
37. *Spanda karika*
38. *Paramartha-sara*

39. *Linga Purana*
40. Somananda, *Shiva Drshti*, I:2
41. *Pratyabijnahridayam*, 1:1
42. Vasugupta, *Spanda Karika*, II:5
43. *Amritanubhav*, I:13, 26-28, 10-12, 34-45, 39-40; from Abhayananda, S., 1989
44. *Ecclesiasticus*, I: 1-6
45. *Proverbs*, 8:22-30
46. Philo, *Quod a Deo somm.*, 19; *de posteritate Caini*, 63; *de vita Mosis*, II:134
47. *The Gospel of John*, 8:54
48. *Ibid.*, 13:40
49. *Ibid.*, 1:1
50. de Barry, William T. (ed.), 1958; p. 415
51. Affifi, A.E., 1939; p. 21
52. *Ibid.*, p. 11
53. *Ibid.*, p. 11
54. *Ibid.*, pp. 10-11
55. *Ibid.*, p. 21
56. Landau, Rom, 1959; pp. 83-84
57. *Ibid.*, p. 83
58. de Barry, William T. (ed.), 1958; pp. 445-446

PART THREE:
THE KNOWLEDGE OF THE SELF

1. Jastrow, Robert, 1978; Introduction
2. Einstein, Albert, quoted by Capek, M., 1961; p. 319
3. Bohm, David & Hiley, B., 1975; pp. 96, 102
4. Shankaracharya, *Atma Bodha*: 8.9
5. Shankaracharya, *Atma Bodha*: 18, 34, 37
6. *Mundaka Upanishad*: 3.2; Mascaro, Juan, 1965
7. Prabhavananda, Swami (trans.), 1947;

8.   Abhayananda, S., *Thomas á Kempis*, 1992;
       pp. 74-75, 78
9.   Plotinus, *Enneads*, II:3:6
10.   *Ibid.*, II:3:7
11.   Nikhilanda, Swami, 1942; pp. 379-380

PART FOUR:
THE WORSHIP OF THE SELF

1.   Shankaracharya, *Vivekachudamani*,
       Prabhavananda, Swami, 1947
2.   *Bhakti Sutras* of Narada, I:1
3.   Ruysbroeck, Jan, *The Sparkling Stone*, X
4.   Kabir, adapted from Shastri, H.P., 1941; p. 49
5.   Abhayananda, S., 1989; *Amritanubhav, IX:* 1, 7,
       12, 13, 15, 28, 29, 30, 35, 36, 38, 39, 40, 41, 42,
       43, 49, 53, 55, 56, 59, 60, 61, 65, 67, 70, 71.
6.   *Ibid., VII:* 240, 135, 143, 144, 146, 163
7.   Nikhilananda, Swami, 1944;
8.   Prabhavananda, Swami, 1947; p. 131
9.   *Tantraloka*
10.   Bernard of Clairvaux, *On The Song Of Songs*,
       Sermon LXXXIV.4
11.   Blackney, R.B., 1941; p. 109
12.   Ruysbroeck, Jan, *The Sparkling Stone*, IV.
13.   Singh, Trilochan, *et al.*, 1960; p. 42
14.   Orr, W.G., 1947; p. 142

BIBLIOGRAPHY

Abhayananda, S., *History Of Mysticism: The Unchanging Testament, Olympia, Wash., Atma Books, 1987, 1994, 1996.*
_____*Jnaneshvar: The Life And Works Of The Celebrated Thirteenth Century Indian Mystic-Poet,* Olympia, Wash., Atma Books, 1989, 1994.
_____*Thomas á Kempis: On The Love Of God,* Olympia, Wash., Atma Books, 1992.
Affifi, Ginestra, *The Nature Of Matter,* Chicago, University of Chicago Press, 1966.
Arberry, A.J., *Sufism: An Account of The Mystics of Islam,* London, George Allen & Unwin, 1950.
Arnold, Edward V., *Roman Stoicism,* Freeport, N.H., Books For Libraries Press, 1971.
Babbitt, Irving, *The Dhammapada,* New York, Oxford University Press, 1936.
Barbour, Ian G., *Issues In Science And Religion,* Englewood Cliffs,   N.J., Prentice-Hall, 1966.
Barnett, Lincoln, *The Universe And Dr. Einstein,* New York, Wm. Morrow & Co., 1948.
Blackney, R.B., *Meister Eckhart, A Modern Translation,* New York,Harper & Bros., 1941.
Bogart, Gregory C., *Astrology And Spiritual Awakening,* Berkeley, Dawn Mountain Press, 1994.
Bohm, David, *Wholeness And The Implicate Order,* London, Routledge & Kegan Paul, 1980.
_____*Causality And Chance In Modern Physics,* London, Routledge & Kegan Paul, 1957.

_____and Hiley, Basil, "*On The Intuitive Understanding Of Non-Locality As Implied By Quantum Theory,*" *Foundations Of Physics,* Vol. V (1975).

Bohr, Neils, *Atomic Physics And Human Knowledge,* New York, Science Editions, 1961.

Calder, Nigel, *The Key To The Universe,* London, British Broadcasting Corp., 1977.

Campbell, Joseph (ed.), *Myths And Symbols In Indian Art And Civilization,* New York, Pantheon Books, 1963.

Capek, M., *The Philosophical Impact Of Contemporary Physics,* Princeton, N.J., D. Van Nostrand, 1961.

Capra, Fritjof, *The Tao Of Physics,* Boulder, Shambhala, 1975.

D'aygalliers, A.W., *Ruysbroeck, The Admirable,* New York, Kennikat Press, 1969.

de Barry, William T. (ed.), *Sources Of Indian Tradition,* New York, Columbia University Press, 1958.

de Broglie, Louis, *The Revolution In Physics,* New York, Noonday Press, 1953.

De Marquette, J., *Introduction To Comparative Mysticism,* New York, Philosophical Library, 1949.

de Riencourt, Amaury, *The Eye Of Shiva,* New York, William Morrow & Co., 1981.

Drennen, D.A. (ed.), *A Modern Introduction To Metaphysics,* New York, Free Press Of Glencoe, 1962.

Durant, Will, *Ceasar And Christ,* New York, Simon & Schuster, 1944.

Gal-Or, Benjamin, *Cosmology, Physics And Philosophy,* New York, Springer-Verlag, 1981.

Gamow, George, *Thirty Years That Shook Physics,*
   New York, Doubleday & Co., 1966.
Guilleman, Victor, *The Story Of Quantum Mechanics,*
   New York, Charles Scribner's Sons, 1968.
Hand, Robert, *Astrological Symbols,* Rockfort, Mass.,
   Para Research, Inc., 1980.
Heisenberg, Werner, *Physics And Philosophy,* New
   York, Harper & Bros., 1958.
Hoffman, Banesh, *The Strange Story Of The Quanta,*
   New York, Dover Publications, 1959.
Huxley, Aldous, *The Perennial Philosophy,* New York,
   World Publishing Co., 1944.
Hyman, A. & Walsh, J., *Philosophy In The Middle Ages,*
   New York, Harper & Row, 1967.
Inge, W.R., *Christian Mysticism,* New York, Meridian
   Books, 1950.
Isherwood, Christopher (ed.), *Vedanta For The   Western
   World,* Hollywood, Vedanta Press, 1946.
Jammer, Max, *Concepts Of Force, A Study In The
   Foundations Of Dynamics,* New York, Harper
   Torchbooks, 1957.
___*The Philosophy Of Quantum Mechanics,* New York,
   John Wiley & Sons, 1974.
Jastrow, Robert, *God And The Astronomers,* New York,
   W.W. Norton & Co., 1978.
Jeans, Sir James, *Physics And Philosophy,* Cambridge,
   Cambridge University Press, 1948.
Jnaneshvar, *Jnaneshvari* (trans. by V.G. Pradhan), 2
   vols., London, George Allen & Unwin, 1969.
Jones, Rufus, *The Flowering Of Mysticism,* New York,
   Macmillan, 1939.

Kadlowbousky, E. & Palmer, G.E.H. (trans.), *The Philokalia,* London, Faber & Faber, 1954.

Katsaros, T. & Kaplan, N., *The Western Mystical Tradition,* Vol. I., New Haven, College & University Press, 1969.

Kirk, K.E., *The Vision Of God,* New York, Harper Torchbooks, 1966.

Landau, Rom, *The Philosophy Of Ibn 'Arabi,* London, George Allen & Unwin, 1959.

Lao Tzu, *The Way And Its Power* (trans. by Arthur Waley), London, 1933.

Lindsay, Jack, *Origins Of Astrology,* New York, Barnes & Noble, Inc., 1971.

Ling, Trevor, *The Buddha,* New York, Chas. Scribner's Sons, 1973.

MacKenna, Stephen (trans.), *Plotinus, The Enneads,* London, Faber & Faber, 1956.

Magill, Frank N. & Mc Greal, I.P., *Masterpieces Of Christian Literature,* New York, Harper & Row, 1963.

Mahadevan, T.M.P., *Ramana Maharshi: The Sage Of Arunachala,* London, George Allen & Unwin, 1977.

_____*Invitation To Indian Philosophy,* New Delhi, Arnold Heinemann, 1974.

Mascaro, Juan (trans.), *Bhagavad Gita,* Middlesex, Penguin Books, 1962.

_____*The Upanishads,* Middlesex, Penguin Books, 1965.

McIntosh, Christopher, *The Astrologers And Their Creed,* London, Hutchinson & Co., 1969.

Muktananda, Swami, *Play Of Consciousness,* South Fallsburg, N.Y., SYDA Foundation, 1978.

___*Secret Of The Siddhas*, Fallsburg, New York, 1980, SYDA Foundation.

Murchie, Guy, *Music Of The Spheres,* New York, Houghton Mifflin, 1961.

Nicholson, Reynold A., *The Mathnawi of Jalal-ud-din Rumi,* 6 vols., London, 1925.

Nikhilananda, Swami (trans.), *The Gospel Of Sri Ramakrishna,* New York, Ramakrishna-Vivekananda Center, 1942.

Orr, W.G., *A Sixteenth Century Indian Mystic,* London, Lutterworth Press, 1947.

Otto, Rudolph, *Mysticism East And West,* New York, Meridian Books, 1957.

Pagels, Heinz R., *The Cosmic Code: Quantum Physics As The Language Of Nature,* New York, Simon & Schuster, 1982.

Petry, Ray C. (ed.), *Late Medieval Mysticism: Vol. XIII of The Library Of Christian Classics,* Philadelphia, Westminster Press, 1957.

Planck, Max, *Where Is Science Going?* London, George Allen & Unwin, 1933.

Prabhavananda, Swami (trans.),*Vivekachudamani by Shankaracharya,* Hollywood, Vedanta Press, 1947.

___*Srimad Bhagavatam, "The Wisdom Of God,"* Madras, Sri Ramakrishna Math, 1978.

___*The Spiritual Heritage Of India,* New York, Doubleday & Co., 1947.

Radhakrishnan, S., *Indian Philosophy,* London, George Allen & Unwin, 1923.

___*Eastern Religions And Western Thought,* London, George Allen & Unwin, 1939.

Ranade, R.D., *Pathway To God In Hindi Literature,*
Bombay, Bharatiya Vidya Bhavan, 1959.

Schimmel, Annemarie, *Mystical Dimensions Of Islam,*
N.C., University of North Carolina Press, 1975.

Shastri, H.P., *Indian Mystic Verse,* London, Shanti Sadan,
1941.

___*Panchadashi by Vidyaranya,* London, Shanti Sadan,
1965.

Singh, Trilochan, *et al* (eds.), *Selections From The
Sacred Writings Of The Sikhs,* London, George
Allen & Unwin, 1960.

Stace, W.T., *The Teaching Of The Mystics,* New York,
Mentor, 1969.

___*Mysticism And Philosophy,* New York, J.B. Lippencott
Co., 1960.

Suzuki, D.T., *Mysticism: Christian & Buddhist,* New
York, Harper & Bros., 1957.

___*Outlines Of Mahayana Buddhism,* New York,
Schocken Books, 1963.

Tagore, Rabindranath, *One Hundred Poems Of Kabir,*
London, 1915.

Tauber, Gerald (ed.), *Albert Einstein's Theory Of
General Relativity,* New York, Crown Publishers, 1979.

Thackston, Wm. Jr. (trans.), *Signs Of The Unseen: The
Discourses of Jalaluddin Rumi,* Putney, Vermont,
Threshold Books, 1994.

Turnbull, Grace H. (ed.), *The Essence Of Plotinus,* based
on the translation of Stephen MacKenna, New York,
Oxford University Press, 1934.

Underhill, Evelyn, *Mysticism,* New York, E.P. Dutton,
1961.

Vivekananda, Swami, *Jnana Yoga,* New York,
Ramakrishna-Vivekananda Center, 1949.

Watts, Alan, *The Supreme Identity*, New York,
Noonday Press, 1957.
___*The Two Hands Of God,* New York, Macmillan
Publishing Co., 1963.
Weinberg, Steven, *The First three Minutes,* New York,
Basic Books, 1977.
White, John (ed.), *The Highest State Of Consciousness*,
New York, Doubleday Anchor, 1972.
Wolfson, Harry A., *Philo: Foundations Of Religious
Philosophy In Judaism, Christianity, and Islam* (2
vols.), Cambridge, Harvard University Press, 1947.
___*The Philosophy Of The Church Fathers,*
Cambridge, Harvard University Press, 1970.
Zolar, *The History Of Astrology,* New York, Arco
Publishing Co.,1972.
Zukav, Gary, *The Dancing Wu Li Masters,* New York,
Bantam Books, 1979.

BOOKS BY S. ABHAYANANDA

THE SUPREME SELF
(2nd Revised Edition)
The timeless secrets of the undivided Reality which is the
universal Self of all.
ISBN0-914557-10-6   215pp. $14.95

HISTORY OF MYSTICISM: *The Unchanging Testament*
(3rd Revised Edition)
The comprehensive history of Enlightenment examining the
lives and teachings of over forty famous world mystics.
ISBN0-914557-09-2   430pp. $19.95

THE WISDOM OF VEDANTA
(2nd Revised Edition)
The non-Dualistic philosophy of Vedanta presented in thirty-
six varied and illuminating Talks.
ISBN0-914557-06-8   340pp. $14.95

*The above titles may be ordered directly from the publisher.
Please include $3.00 Shipping & handling for the 1st book
and $.50 for each additional book to:*

ATMA BOOKS
3430 Pacific Ave. S.E.
Suite A-6144
Olympia, WA 98501

This book was typeset on a Macintosh Performa 575 computer, utilizing Word 5.1 software. The text was set in 12 pt. Garamond Roman FLF; the titles were set in 18 pt. Present font. It was printed by Thomson-Shore, Inc. of Dexter, Mich.